Heavenly Cooking

Heavenly C🌐🌐king

from

SPACE CITY U★S★A

All Recipes Home-Tested

Compiled by
the Members of the Sisterhood of
TEMPLE BETH ISRAEL
Houston, Texas

Illustrations by Mrs. Si Sartorius

FIRST EDITION 1967

Press of Premier

HOUSTON, TEXAS

FOREWORD

Dr. Hyman Judah Schachtel

Chief Rabbi, Congregation Beth Israel

"And thou shall eat and be satisfied, and bless the Lord, thy God for the good land which He has given thee." Dt. 8:10

The good food we eat is a blessing from the Lord, our God. Judaism, a religion of this world, teaches us to appreciate the gifts of the earth and all the reasonable pleasures of life. Our food which sustains us can also delight us. It is one of the arts of living for which we thank God.

When we sit down to eat we offer gratitude to God in the benediction, "Blessed art Thou, O Lord our God, King of the Universe, who bringeth forth bread from the earth." By reciting this grace before meals we are constantly made aware of our obligation to express our love for God in every act of life. The daily meals, the Sabbath banquet, the special feasts of the Holy Days and Festivals are surrounded by prayers which transform the dining table into a miniature altar.

Let us see in this cookbook, gathered from the tasty recipes offered by members of our Sisterhood, a contribution to the enjoyment of living, and a tribute to God from whom all blessings flow.

May this collection of recipes bring pleasure to all who use it, and abiding satisfaction to those who have made it possible.

EDITOR'S LETTER

Just as the secrets behind Space Conquest are carefully guarded, so are the recipes of the creative cook. I am deeply grateful to the many women who shared their culinary best with us and wish so much that it had been possible to use them all.

For two years, a devoted committee of women have spent innumerable hours in a labor of love to create this book. I should like to take this opportunity to thank those too numerous to name, who typed, phoned, and contributed their time to our efforts. A very special thank you to the ladies listed below whose responsibilities were great and whose achievements have exceeded my greatest ambitions for *Heavenly Cooking from Space City, U.S.A.*

Editor
Mrs. Gerald L. Katz (Doris)

Assistant Editors
Mrs. Charles Freundlich (Bette)
Mrs. Sam Levy (Janis)

Art and Illustrations
Mrs. Si Sartorius (Bunny)

Typing
Mrs. L. M. Landa, Jr. (Lois)
Mrs. Charles Hanovice (Kay)

Production
Mrs. Milton Gugenheim (Aileen)

Sales and Publicity
Mrs. Carl Herman, Jr. (Gloria)
Mrs. Raymond Kaufman (Cookie)
Mrs. M. M. Lewis (Grace)

Financial Secretary
Mrs. I. Mark Westheimer (Gerry)

Sisterhood President
Mrs. Melvin Maltz (Phyllis)

Commentary
Mrs. Henry Wexner, Jr. (Ellen)

Recipe Testing and Gathering
Mrs. Simon Frank (Hank)
Mrs. Jerry Rubenstein (Linda)

Mrs. Sam Simkin (Helen)
Mrs. John Landa (Nancy)

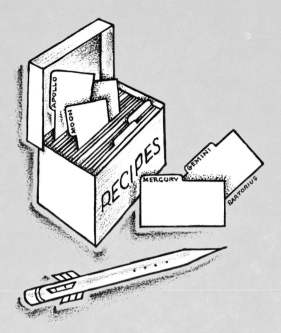

B. Sartorius

APPETIZERS

ANTIPASTO

1 bottle catsup
1 bottle chili sauce
Worcestershire sauce to taste
beef-steak sauce to taste
A-1 sauce to taste
walnut sauce to taste
few drops tabasco
1 large can white tuna

1 large can small drained
   mushrooms
1 large can pitted ripe olives
1 jar small artichoke hearts
raw cauliflower heads
sliced dill pickles
1 can small sardines

Divide tuna into small pieces. Cut olives, artichokes, mushrooms, cauliflower, pickles, and sardines into tiny pieces. Mix above with chili sauce. Sprinkle rest of sauces over all.

This mixture may be frozen in small containers and thawed several hours before using.

Serves 6 - 8.

Mrs. Henry Desenberg (Helen)

HERRING MOLD

1 - 8 ounce jar herring
   (skinned and boned)
1 small can white tuna fish
1 small bottle pimento olives,
   chopped
¼ pound butter
1 envelope gelatin

dash of tabasco
Worcestershire sauce (several
   spoons)
lemon juice (about 1
   tablespoon)
onion juice (if desired)

Grind herring, tuna and 5 or 6 black pepper corns. Cream butter until soft, add to herring, tuna, olives and seasonings. Soak 1 envelope gelatin in a little herring juice, add a little boiling water, stir until dissolved. Put a small amount of gelatin in bottom of a fish mold to set for glaze. Mix remaining gelatin well into all other ingredients. Pour into mold.

Mrs. A. F. Miller (Flora)

5

MARINATED BEEF SLICES

1 pound well done beef tender
   sliced thin and long
1½ cups sour cream
Sauce:
lemon peel to taste

2 tablespoons horseradish
a few drops Worcestershire
   sauce
salt and pepper
1 large onion, chopped

Mix well, then add 1½ cups sour cream. Pour over meat. Serve on individual small plates.

Stockyards Inn Chicago

Mrs. Joel Levy (Tudy)

CRAB MEAT BALINESE

1 pound crab meat (either dark
   or white)
2 eggs

1 tablespoon flour
1 pound bacon

Mix crab meat, flour, well beaten eggs and season with salt, garlic powder and Louisiana hot sauce. Roll this in individual portions in strips of thin sliced bacon and run under broiler until bacon is crisp. Serve hot with Hollandaise sauce.

Mrs. William Ladin (Lois)

RED CAVIAR DIP

¼ pound red caviar
1 cup sour cream
1 - 3 ounce package cream
   cheese, softened

Season to taste with:
salt
onion juice
garlic powder
lemon juice
Worcestershire sauce

Mix all ingredients except caviar, which should be added last. Chill.

Mrs. Si Sartorius (Bunny)

SOUR CREAM HERRING APPETIZER

1 pint herring in wine sauce,
   drained, cut in small pieces
½ pint sour cream
½ cup mayonnaise
juice of one lemon
1 teaspoon celery seed

1 bunch chopped green onions
   (slice tops fine)
¾ teaspoon chopped green
   pepper (optional)
1 tablespoon sugar

Blend all ingredients thoroughly and chill overnight. Serve with crackers or party rye.

Mrs. R. Goldstein (Harriet)

GUACAMOLE DIP

2 medium sized ripe avocados
1 - 3 ounce package chive
   cheese
1 tablespoon grated onion

juice of one lemon
salt and white pepper to taste
3 or 4 drops tabasco

Mix altogether in mixmaster—chill—put seeds of avocado in mixture to keep green.

Mrs. Frank Falkstein (Farnese)

CHEESE BALL — I

1 pkg. sharp cheese
1 pkg. blue cheese
1 large cream cheese
1 nippy cheese roll
8 slices process Swiss

1 chive cheese
1 garlic cheese roll
1 can parsley flakes
tabasco, paprika, red pepper
juice of garlic and onion

Mix well and roll into desired size balls. Roll in paprika and parsley flakes. May be made early and put in deep freeze.

Mrs. Sam Weiss (Lil)

CHEESE BALL — II

1 - 8 ounce cream cheese
1 - 5 ounce Old English sharp
   cheese
1 - 6 ounce rolled smoked
   cheese
1 teaspoon accent
1 clove garlic, crushed or ¼
   teaspoon garlic powder

1 tablespoon Worcestershire
   sauce
⅛ teaspoon tabasco
1 cup parsley, chopped fine
1 cup chopped pecans
chili powder—sprinkle lightly

Mix half parsley and chopped pecans with cheese, and other ingredients. Then roll cheese ball in remaining parsley and nuts.

Serves 8.

Mrs. Alan Gold (Carol)

CHEESE BALL — III

½ pound cheddar cheese,
   grated fine
1 - 3 ounce package cream
   cheese
4-5 tablespoons dry sherry
½ cup finely chopped ripe
   olives

1 teaspoon Worcestershire
   sauce
dash of onion, garlic, and
   celery salt
package dried chipped beef

Beat all except chipped beef together in mixmaster. Shape into a ball. Wrap in foil and place in ice box. Before serving, roll cheese ball into ½ cup finely chopped dried chipped beef. Pack beef around ball, pressing it to get all of beef around cheese. Double for sizeable amount.

Mrs. A. F. Miller (Flora)

CHEESE SURPRISES

1 stick margarine
½ pound sharp or mild cheese, grated
1½ cups flour

¼ - ½ teaspoon tabasco sauce
dash of garlic salt
small size stuffed olives

Have butter and cheese at room temperature. Blend together with fingertips. Add flour gradually, blend well. Add garlic salt and tabasco and mix well. Break off small bits and flatten in palm of hand, using just enough to wrap completely around an olive. Bake on ungreased cookie sheet at 375° about 15 minutes, or until lightly colored but not browned.

Yield—50 olives.   *Mrs. Cecil Weil (Maxine)*

PINEAPPLE CHEESE SPREAD

top of fresh pineapple
1 pound New York sharp Cheddar cheese
½ pound Roquefort cheese
2 - 4 ounce packages cream cheese
½ pound Swiss cheese
½ pound Jack cheese

½ cup melted butter
juice of 2 limes
½ cup dry sherry
2 tablespoons Worcestershire
1 teaspoon cayenne
1 teaspoon monosodium glutamate
paprika

Cut pineapple top off with a point at bottom to insert in cheese. Grate and mash cheese. Add butter and rest of ingredients, except paprika. Sprinkle paprika all over cheese molded to resemble a pineapple. Cut hole for pineapple top. Use spoon to make indentations like a pineapple. Fix a day before serving.

Serves 24.   *Mrs. Jay Cohen (Helene)*

CHEESE CRUNCHIES

1 jar sharp cheese
½ stick butter
Mix together well and add:

½ cup sifted flour
½ teaspoon salt
¼ teaspoon cayenne pepper

Mix and make into 1 inch balls. Put on greased cookie sheets and refrigerate at least 2 - 3 hours. Bake in 400° oven for 10 minutes. Can be frozen and used whenever necessary.

Serve with drinks before dinner.   *Mrs. Leon Friedlander (Reba)*

CURRIED CRAB MEAT SPREAD

2 large (8 ounce) packages
  cream cheese
3 tablespoons mayonnaise
lemon juice to taste
Worcestershire to taste
½ teaspoon grated onion

paprika
½ teaspoon salt
½ teaspoon red pepper
½ teaspoon curry powder
1 can crab meat to be added to
  above

Mix all ingredients in a mixer then add crab meat which has been boned well. Grease a small mold and pack with above mixture. Refrigerate. For use in a fish mold, triple recipe.

Mrs. DeWitt Grossman (Lois)

PARMESAN CHEESE CRAB MEAT APPETIZER

bread rounds
3 tablespoons margarine
3 tablespoons flour
¾ cup milk
¼ cup cream
¾ cup grated baby eye Swiss
  cheese

3 tablespoons dry white wine
salt and fresh ground pepper
¼ teaspoon nutmeg
½ cup lump crab meat
grated parmesan cheese

Cut bread with biscuit cutter and butter on both sides. Put in slow oven and dry out like melba toast. Turn once.

Melt margarine, add flour, milk and cream to make a sauce. When thick and cool, add Swiss cheese, wine, seasoning and fold in crab meat. Sprinkle with grated parmesan cheese. Broil until brown.

Mrs. Michael Spolane (Renie)

GEFILTE FISH

10 pounds of fish. (Have market skin, bone, and fillet fish. We use Red Fisn or Red and Trout or Red and Red Snapper.)

6-8 eggs	⅔ cup of Matzo meal (Passover)
2 large onions	or cracker meal
3 or 4 carrots	water to keep moist
3 or 4 stalks of celery	salt and pepper to taste
parsley	

Put fish fillets through the grinder. Add one onion that has previously been chopped into small pieces, into grinder with fish.

After grinding put in a wooden chop bowl and add eggs one at a time while chopping the fish. Keep adding water to keep fish moist and light so it will not pack. The more air chopped into fish the better the texture.

While preparing fish take the heads, bones, skin, onion, carrots, celery, parsley, salt, and pepper. Put in large soup-kettle and fill with enough water to allow all this to cook about one hour. Strain out all fish bones and vegetables and let come to a boil again. Drop in the fish balls, taste both fish and stock to see it is properly seasoned. Moisten hands and form balls lightly, drop in boiling water. Cook 1½ to 2 hours. Pour stock over fish and let stand over night to jell. (Serve hot or cold.)

Yield—15 to 20.

Mrs. B. Block
Mrs. Albert Meyerson
Mrs. L. M. Landa, Sr.

11

PIZZA

Crust:
1 package active dry yeast
1¼ cups warm water
2 tablespoons vegetable oil
4 cups flour
1 teaspoon salt
Tomato sauce:
1 - 15-ounce can tomato sauce
1 - 12-ounce can tomato paste
2½ cups water
1 teaspoon salt
¼ teaspoon pepper
1½ teaspoons oregano
1½ teaspoons Italian seasoning

¼ teaspoon garlic powder
Topping:
½ pound pan sausage, cooked
    and drained of grease
8 ounces pepperoni
1 medium onion, chopped
1 medium green pepper,
    chopped
1 can mushrooms
1 pound Mozzarella cheese,
    sliced thin or shredded
Parmesan cheese
anchovies (optional)

Dissolve 1 package active yeast in 1¼ cups warm water. Stir in 2 tablespoons vegetable oil. Sift flour and salt together. Stir into oil water mixture, knead vigorously in cloth or on board until smooth and elastic, about 15 minutes. Shape into ball; place in greased bowl; brush with oil; cover with damp cloth. Let rise until double in bulk, about 2 hours. Form again into ball. (Makes enough for four pizzas.) Cut dough into four pieces. Roll each piece into 10″ circle. Fit into 4 pie tins; brush with oil.

Sauce: Combine all ingredients in heavy sauce pan and simmer for 2 hours. Add more water if necessary. Spoon into dough in pizza pans.

Spread topping ingredients over pizza sauce in order given. Sprinkle with Parmesan. Bake in 450° oven for 15 minutes or until dough is brown and crisp.

Other toppings:

Ground beef sauteed with seasoned salt and seasoned pepper in place of sausage.

Hot dog chunks (cooked).

Mrs. Robert E. Caine (Sunny L.)

HOT SHRIMP APPETIZER

2 pounds cooked and cleaned
   shrimp
½ cup melted butter
2 mashed garlic cloves

¼ cup chopped parsley
¼ teaspoon paprika
¼ cup cooking sherry
1 cup bread crumbs

Add seasoning to melted butter. Stir in sherry. Toss with bread crumbs. Place shrimp in shells or ramekins. Spoon crumbs over shrimp. Bake 20 minutes in 325° oven. Sprinkle with parsley. Serve hot.

Serves 4 - 6.

Mrs. Ronny Finger (Judy)

PICKLED SHRIMP APPETIZER

2½ to 3 pounds shrimp boiled
   in seasoned water or crab
   boil
celery tops
boil 10 to 12 minutes
Sauce:
1¼ cups cooking oil

¾ cup vinegar
1½ teaspoons salt
2½ teaspoons celery seed
2½ tablespoons capers and juice
dash tabasco
sliced onions
7 to 8 bay leaves

In a glass jar alternate shrimp and sliced onions. Top with seven or eight bay leaves. Place cover tight on jar. Let marinate two days.

Serves 8 to 10 people.

Mrs. Louis Leon (Bertha)

SARDINE FINGERS

1 can sardines
2 packages cream cheese
½ teaspoon baking powder

1 teaspoon onion juice
1 egg yolk
salt and paprika

Mix all ingredients together. Cut bread in finger shapes, toast on one side. Place skinless and boneless sardine on untoasted side. Spread mixture on top. Sprinkle with paprika, place in hot oven until puffed and brown.

Mrs. Sam Weiss (Lil)

SNACKS FOR COCKTAIL TIME

½ cup butter
½ cup bacon drippings
1 tablespoon Worcestershire
1 tablespoon seasoned salt
2 tablespoons tabasco sauce

1 tablespoon garlic salt
2 - 8 ounce cans salted nuts
1 box cheerios (medium)
1 box rice chex (medium)
1 box pretzel sticks (medium)

Mix all ingredients in large roaster pan and cook in 200° oven, stirring often, for one hour. Makes about 1 gallon.

Mrs. Frank Falkstein (Farnice)

STUFFED TOMATO SNACK

8 cherry tomatoes
2 egg yolks, hard boiled
4 anchovies
1 tablespoon capers
1 teaspoon mustard

1 tablespoon cognac
olive oil (to make smooth)
1 teaspoon mayonnaise
salt and cayenne pepper to taste

Cut off tops of tomatoes and drain. Mash egg yolk. Mix all together until smooth. Place mixture in tomatoes. Top each with slice of olive.

Serves 3 - 4.   *Mrs. Sydney Cohen (Harriet)*

PICKLED BLACK-EYED PEAS

2 cans dried black-eyed peas
¼ cup salad oil
½ cup vinegar
2 cloves garlic

1 onion sliced thin
1 teaspoon salad black pepper
1 teaspoon oregano
2 bay leaves

Drain liquid from peas. Place in bowl. Add remaining ingredients and mix well. Store in jar in ice box for 2 days. Excellent at cocktail parties or used as a relish.

Serves 8.   *Mrs. Robert Rappold (Elizabeth)*

MARINATED OLIVES

1 can (7 oz.) extra large pitted
   ripe olives
1 can (2 oz.) anchovy fillets cut
   in ⅓ pieces
1 can (4 oz.) pimento, chopped

1 clove garlic, mashed
⅓ cup wine vinegar
1 tablespoon olive oil
¼ cup chopped parsley

Drain olives and anchovies. Save oil from anchovies. Stuff olives with anchovy pieces. Place in bowl. Season olives with mixture of chopped pimento, garlic, wine vinegar, olive oil, and oil from anchovies. Cover. Let stand over night, turning olives several times in marinade. Add parsley to mixture about 30 minutes before serving.

Mrs. Simon Frank (Hank)

RUMAKI

½ pound chicken livers
1½ tablespoons honey
1 tablespoon soy sauce
2 tablespoons cooking oil
½ clove garlic, crushed

1 - 5 ounce can water chestnuts,
   drained
18 slices bacon, cut in halves or
   thirds

Rinse chicken livers with cold water; drain on absorbent paper. Cut in quarters and put into a bowl. Pour a mixture of honey, soy sauce, cooking oil and garlic over livers; cover. Let stand about 30 minutes, turning pieces occasionally. Remove livers from marinade and drain on absorbent paper. Cut each water chestnut into quarters. Wrap a piece of bacon around a piece of chicken liver and a piece of water chestnut; secure with a wooden pick. Arrange appetizers on broiler rack and place in broiler with tops of appetizers about 2" from source of heat. Broil, turning once with tongs, about 10 minutes, or until bacon is cooked. Serve hot.

Yield—3 dozen.
   Mrs. Frank Herzog (Dorene)

BROILED STUFFED MUSHROOMS

12 large fresh mushrooms
trim off tips of stems
remove caps (if they are extra
large, pour boiling water
over and let stand for one
minute)
chop stems very fine

Stuffing:
½ cup crab meat (boned)
snipped into fine pieces

cook chopped mushroom stems
in 1 tablespoon butter or
margarine until tender, do
not brown
add crab meat
add ¼ cup finely chopped celery
add 2 tablespoons mayonnaise
or salad dressing
add 1 teaspoon fresh lemon
juice
dash of salt

Stuff caps; sprinkle tops with 2 tablespoons fine dry bread crumbs mixed with 1 tablespoon melted butter.

Broil 6 inches from heat about 10 minutes after guests arrive so these appetizers are sizzling. Serve with forks.

Mrs. Ross Seline (Dee)

ITALIAN STUFFED MUSHROOMS

1½ pounds mushrooms (large,
even-sized)
⅓ cup grated Parmesan cheese
½ cup dry bread crumbs
¼ cup grated onion
2 cloves garlic, minced

2 tablespoons minced parsley
½ teaspoon salt
¼ teaspoon freshly ground
black pepper
½ teaspoon oregano
⅓ cup vegetable oil

Wash mushrooms in water with a little lemon juice; dry. Remove the stems and chop; mix with the cheese, bread crumbs, onion, garlic, parsley, salt, pepper, and oregano. Stuff the mushroom caps with this mixture. Pour a little oil in a baking pan. Arrange mushrooms in it. Pour remaining oil over them. Bake at 350° for 25 minutes.

Serves 6 - 8.   *Mrs. Gene Burke (Jean)*

PATE ASPIC MINIATURES

1 envelope unflavored gelatin
1 can condensed beef consomme
3 tablespoons water
stuffed olives (a few)
1 can (4½ ozs.) liver pate
1 can (4½ ozs.) deviled ham

1 - 3 ounce package cream
  cheese
½ teaspoon anchovy paste
½ grated onion
24 melba toast rounds

Soften gelatin in water, add to hot consomme, remove from heat. Grease miniature muffin tins (to hold 24) lightly with salad oil and spoon in 1 teaspoon gelatin mixture. When almost set, place 1 slice of olive in each. Mix liver pate, deviled ham, onion and ¼ cup of gelatin mixture, add layer in each cup, chill; then add another layer of the following mixture: softened cream cheese, anchovy paste and small amount gelatin mixture. Let set. Finish filling cups with gelatin mixture, and chill. Just before serving loosen each mold around edge with knife, lift out carefully. Place each mold on melba toast rounds when ready to serve.

Yield—24.   *Mrs. Si Sartorius (Bunny)*

SWEET AND SOUR MEATBALLS

2 pounds ground chuck
2 slices bread (soak in water
  and squeeze water out)
salt, pepper, accent, chili
  powder, Worcestershire to
  taste

butter for browning
Sauce:
1 bottle chili sauce
1 jar grape jelly
juice of one lemon

Combine meat with all other ingredients, season heavily. Shape into miniature meatballs and brown in butter.

Combine sauce ingredients in saucepan and heat. Add meatballs and heat again to use.

Yield—100.   *Mrs. Leo Rose (Chickie)*

17

LIVER PATE FRANCAIS

1 teaspoon rendered chicken fat
1 egg
¼ cup good cognac
¾ cup heavy whipping cream
1 pound chicken livers (raw)
⅓ cup fresh unrendered
   chicken fat, diced

1 small onion, coarsely chopped
¼ cup flour
2½ teaspoons salt
½ teaspoon ground ginger
1 teaspoon white pepper
½ teaspoon allspice

Grease 1½ quart mold or loaf pan with unrendered chicken fat. Place egg, cognac, and cream in blender, and blend chicken livers gradually, diced fat, onion and flour until finely pureed. It may be necessary to do in small installments. To the puree, add all seasonings and mix well. Pour into mold, cover top with double thickness of foil. Place in pan of water and bake at 325° for 1¼ hours. Cool, then store in refrigerator. If desired may be decorated with truffles and clear aspic poured over liver pate. Serve with toast rounds or crackers.

Mrs. Ben Wolfman (*Mildred*)

CRAB MEAT IN RAMEKINS

1 pound lump crab meat
½ cup cream sauce
½ tablespoon lemon juice
1 tablespoon horseradish
1 egg, beaten

2 tablespoons parsley
2 tablespoons catsup
salt, pepper, and Worcestershire sauce to taste
buttered bread crumbs

Mix crab meat and other ingredients lightly together. Fill ramekins, sprinkle with crumbs and bake until brown, 10 - 12 minutes. This mixture may also be molded and put on an artichoke bottom and baked.

Serves 4.

Mrs. Irvin Shlenker (*Bertha Alyce*)

SOPAS (Mexican appetizer or snack)

1 medium onion
1 medium tomato
2 or 3 Jalapenos

¾ pound American cheese
1 large package round corn
  chips

Brown chopped onion in salad oil. Add tomato that has been peeled and chopped with chopped Jalapenos. Then stir in cheese that has been coarsely grated. When cheese is melted fold in corn chips and serve immediately.

Mrs. Si Sartorius (Bunny)

EGGS, PANCAKES, BREAD and ROLLS

CHEESE APPLE BLINTZES

Filling:
1 - 8 ounce package shredded
   cheddar cheese
2 tablespoons butter
2 cups finely chopped apple
1 tablespoon sugar
¼ teaspoon cinnamon

1 tablespoon grated lemon peel
Batter:
¾ cup sifted flour
¼ teaspoon salt
⅔ cup water
2 eggs
½ cup milk

To prepare filling: Pan fry apples in butter, and add sugar, cinnamon and lemon peel. Cook a few minutes to blend flavors.

To make batter: Mix together flour and salt. Add water, mixing to smooth paste. Add eggs and beat. Blend in milk.

Make blintze in small pan which has been heated first and then greased.

Yields 15.   *Mrs. Morey Miller (Mae)*

CHEESE BLINTZES — I

Batter:
3 large eggs well beaten
1 cup sifted flour
1 scant teaspoon salt
(approx.) 1½ cup milk and
   water mixed

Filling:
1 pound dry cottage cheese
1 package cream cheese
2 tablespoons melted butter
1 tablespoon sugar
2 egg yolks

Press cheese through colander, salt to taste—add other ingredients. Make batter by adding salt and liquid to well beaten eggs. Add flour and stir until smooth. Strain. Lightly grease 6 or 7 inch cast iron griddle (I use cooking oil on a paper towel) and heat thoroughly but not smoking. Pour quickly a scant ¼ cup batter, tilting griddle from side to side so a very thin pancake covers entire bottom. Bake a few seconds until bottom sets. Toss baked side up on a clean towel on a board. Proceed until all batter is baked. Then place a spoon of cheese mixture at one end of pancake, fold over sides, then end and fold envelope style. Fry in butter before serving.

Mrs. G. Frank Lipper (Nanette)

CHEESE BLINTZES — II

Pancakes:
2 eggs
⅛ teaspoon salt
¾ cup sifted flour
1 cup milk

Filling:
1 pound dry cottage cheese
½ teaspoon salt
1 egg
2 teaspoons sugar

Pancakes:

Beat eggs well and add salt and flour at one time. Add milk gradually and beat smooth until batter is very thin. Use small teflon skillet, lightly greased. Pour 2 tablespoons of batter in skillet to cover bottom of pan. Fry until lightly browned on bottom and turn out, fried side up, on board.

Blend all ingredients for filling together.

Fill pancake with 1 tablespoon of filling and fold into shape of envelope. Before serving, fry both sides until golden brown. Serve hot with sour cream, preserves, or sugar.

Yield—one dozen.   *Mrs. David Brand (Mollie)*

GERMAN PANCAKES

4 eggs
4 tablespoons flour
1½ tablespoons sugar
½ cup milk
1 pinch salt
½ stick margarine

1 lemon, juice only
¼ cup sugar
¼ teaspoon cinnamon
½ stick margarine
powdered sugar

Heat oven to 425°. Beat eggs, flour, sugar, milk, and salt. Heat a frying pan with margarine, melt but don't brown. Add batter to skillet and bake 7 minutes. Reduce heat to 375°, bake 8 minutes more. Dot with margarine, dust with sugar and cinnamon and sprinkle with lemon juice. Roll up and place on hot platter. Dust with powdered sugar and serve at once.

Serves 6.   *Mrs. Melvin Maltz (Phyllis)*

FRENCH PANCAKES

6 eggs
2 tablespoons sugar
6 tablespoons melted butter

1 quart milk
2 scant cups of sifted cake flour

Beat whole eggs till light and fluffy, stir in sugar. Add melted butter, milk and flour last. Drop by tablespoons into small pan greased with butter and cook slowly. May be served with preserves or jellies.

Mrs. Gerald Katz (Doris)

MATZO PANCAKES (Eierkuchen)

4 eggs
½ cup milk

½ cup matzo meal

Mix yolks, milk and meal. Add beaten whites. Fry in butter until golden brown. Serve with sugar or syrup.

Serves 4.   *Mrs. Charles Newman (Diane)*

MOTHER'S MATZO PANCAKES

5 large or 10 small tea matzos
milk
4 eggs
4 tablespoons sugar

cinnamon
2 tablespoons butter
⅛ pound slivered almonds
1 tablespoon sugar

Soak matzos in enough milk to cover. Soak at least 3 hours or even over night in ice box. Mash and drain them in a colander. Beat 1 whole egg and 3 egg yolks for a very long time. Add 4 tablespoons sugar. Add cinnamon and melted butter, then add the almonds. Beat 3 egg whites until stiff. Add 1 tablespoon sugar. Fold whites into mixture and fry in butter slowly. Serve with sugar or strawberry preserves.

Mrs. Abe Zuber (Stella)

QUICHE ADELE

1 ten inch pie shell
5 or 6 eggs (according to size)
¾ cup milk

1¼ cup grated Gruyere cheese
1 cup slivered corn beef or lean
ham

Beat eggs and milk from one to two minutes. Fold in meat and cheese. Pour into pre-baked pie shell and bake until golden in 400° oven. Let set 30 to 40 minutes before serving.

Mrs. Bernard Perlmutter (Adele)

QUICHE LORRAINE

pastry for 9-inch pie shell
¼ pound bacon
4 eggs
1¾ cups light cream

1 teaspoon salt
pinch cayenne pepper
½ pound grated Swiss cheese

Line pie tin with pastry, flute edges. Chill in refrigerator, if possibly overnight. Fry bacon crisp, drain off all grease on paper towel. Beat eggs lightly, add cream and seasoning. Crumble bacon to cover bottom of pie tin, spread grated Swiss cheese over bacon. Pour egg mixture over cheese. Bake at 400° for 35-45 minutes (until silver knife comes clean). Cool 7 minutes on wire rack and serve cut in wedges.

Mrs. Albert A. Kaufman (Jean)

CHEESE SOUFFLE — I

4 tablespoons butter
1 cup milk
4 tablespoons flour
½ teaspoon salt

few grains cayenne pepper
½ cup grated cheese
4 egg yolks beaten very light
4 egg whites beaten *very stiff*

Melt butter, add flour, add milk, and stir until thick and smooth. Add salt, pepper, and cheese. (Make sauce on slow fire and stir well.) Remove from fire, add yolks, pour into whites. Pour into buttered baking dish, bake 25 minutes in 325° oven.

Mrs. Simon Sakowitz (Clara)

CHEESE SOUFFLE — II

¾ pound sharp cheddar cheese
salt and pepper
6 eggs

2 cups milk
⅛ pound butter
8 slices bread

Cut off crusts of bread and cut into cubes. Grate cheese coarsely. Beat eggs well. Add salt, pepper and milk. Melt butter and add to above. Alternate bread and cheese in unbuttered casserole or pan. Pour liquid over all. Refrigerate overnight. Next day, bake 1 hour at 350°.

Serves 8.　　*Mrs. Wm. Boas* given by *Mrs. Chas. Freundlich (Bette)*

CRISP WAFFLES

2 cups cake flour
4 teaspoons baking powder
½ teaspoon salt
1 tablespoon sugar
1 cup milk

½ cup cream
2 egg yolks
⅔ cup melted butter
2 stiffly beaten egg whites

Sift flour, baking powder, salt and sugar. Add milk and cream slowly, beating till smooth. Add 2 beaten yolks, then melted butter and fold in stiffly beaten egg whites last. Bake in hot waffle iron.

Mrs. Gerald Katz (Doris)

POTATO PANCAKES — I

1½ medium potatoes per person
1 tablespoon vinegar
1 egg per potato
salt and pepper

¼ teaspoon grated onion per
    potato
shortening

Pare potatoes and soak in cold water with the vinegar about 30 minutes. Grate on large size grater onto paper towels. Be sure potatoes are dry. Add eggs, salt, pepper and grated onion. Mix well. Fry in shortening until golden brown.

Mrs. Frank Falkstein (Farnese)

POTATO PANCAKES — II

5 large Idaho potatoes, peeled
5 eggs, beaten
1 medium size onion
1 teaspoon baking powder
2 tablespoons flour

1 tablespoon cracker or matzo
    meal
shortening
salt and pepper

Submerge potatoes in cold water for 30 minutes. (Makes grating easier.) Drain, pat dry. Grate potatoes by hand, on fine side of grater. Drain off water. Grate onion. Combine potatoes, onion and eggs, then the sifted dry ingredients mixing well. In a large skillet, over medium heat, melt enough shortening for 1 inch depth. Drop potato mixture from a tablespoon into hot shortening, allowing several tablespoons for each pancake, depending on desired size. Turn when edge is golden brown. Turn only once. Drain on paper towel. Add additional shortening as needed.

Serves 4.

Mrs. William Gold (Lillyan)

TEA BISCUITS

2 cups sifted flour
3 teaspoons baking powder
   (single action)
½ teaspoon salt

2-4 tablespoons sugar (can be
   omitted)
6 tablespoons shortening
1 egg and milk to make ⅔ cup

Mix dry ingredients together. Cut in shortening. Add egg and milk. Place on floured board and knead for 30 seconds. Roll and cut. Brush top of biscuits with melted butter. Bake on greased pan in 450° oven 10 - 12 minutes. Makes 24 small biscuits.

Mr. and Mrs. Jules Breitenbach

SPOON BREAD

1 cup white cornmeal
1 cup water
2 eggs

1 teaspoon sugar
1 teaspoon salt
1 tablespoon shortening

Heat cornmeal, milk and water on low fire until mush. Turn off fire. Add 2 egg yolks, sugar, salt and stir well. Melt shortening in baking dish. Beat egg whites stiff, fold in cornmeal mixture. Bake in 350° preheated oven for 30 to 40 minutes or until browned on top. Use 2½ quart dish.

Serves 4.

Mrs. Mamie Alexander

CHEESE STRAWS

1 pound New York sharp
   cheese
1 stick margarine

2 cups flour
red pepper
salt

Combine ingredients and bake on a cookie sheet. This can be made in a roll and sliced or squirted through a cookie press.

Mrs. S. J. Weiss (Lil)

29

MEXICAN CORN BREAD

1½ cups yellow corn meal
2 eggs
⅔ cup oil
1 cup sour cream
1 cup cream style corn
3 teaspoons baking powder

1 teaspoon salt
3 small Jalapeno peppers, chopped
1 cup grated yellow cheddar cheese

Mix as any other cornbread. Pour ½ batter in hot greased pan. Cover with half grated cheese. Pour rest of batter in the pan. Sprinkle with remaining cheese. Bake in 350° oven for 35 minutes in 8 x 10 pan.

Mrs. B. G. Winner (Irene)

BANANA BREAD

1¼ cup flour
1 teaspoon soda
½ teaspoon salt
1 cup sugar
½ cup butter

3 mashed bananas
2 eggs, beaten
1 teaspoon vanilla
½ cup nuts, optional

Sift first 4 ingredients and crumble in butter. Mix bananas, beaten eggs and vanilla and add to dry mixture. Add nuts if using. Pour into greased and floured regular bread pan; bake at 325° for 40 minutes.

Mrs. N. Levy (Tillie)

DATE NUT BREAD

1½ cups boiling water
1½ cups chopped dates
2 tablespoons butter
1 egg
1½ cups sugar
1 teaspoon salt

2¾ cups flour
1 teaspoon soda
1 teaspoon cream of tartar
1 cup chopped nuts
1 teaspoon vanilla

Pour boiling water over chopped dates. Add butter, sugar, and salt. Mix and cool. Add well beaten egg and vanilla. Add dry ingredients and nuts. Bake in 350° oven for 50 minutes.

Makes 2 medium sized loaves.   *Mrs. Joel Levy (Tudy)*

LEMON BREAD

1 cup sugar
½ pound butter
3 eggs
1 ounce bottle lemon extract
2 cups flour

1 teaspoon baking powder,
   slightly heaping
¼ teaspoon salt
½ pound white raisins
2 cups broken nut meats

Mix butter and sugar together; add eggs and lemon extract. Combine flour, baking powder and salt. Add raisins and nuts to flour mixture. Combine flour mixture with butter mixture. Line bottom and sides of loaf pan 11 x 5 x 3 with wax paper. Bake at 275° 1½ hours or longer over pan of water which is placed on rack below bread pan. Let stand for a day. Thick slices are better. Wrap in foil.

Serves 15 average size portions.   *Mrs. Jake B. Sampson (Pauline)*

MATZO MEAL ROLLS

½ cup oil
2 cups matzo meal
2 cups boiling water

dash salt and pepper
5 eggs

Stir oil into matzo meal until mixed very thoroughly. Add boiling water, salt and pepper. Stir eggs into matzo meal mixture. Shape into rolls. Place on greased baking sheet which has been sprinkled with matzo meal. Bake 15 to 20 minutes in 400° oven.

Yield: 12 big fluffy rolls.   *Mrs. David Dochen (Sharon)*

ICEBOX ROLLS

1 cup mashed potatoes
⅔ cup shortening
⅔ cup sugar
1 teaspoon salt
1 cup scalded milk

1 yeast cake
½ cup lukewarm water
3 cups flour
5 eggs

Pour scalded milk over potatoes, shortening, sugar and salt. Dissolve yeast cake in lukewarm water and add to cooled milk mixture. Add 3 cups flour, 2 beaten eggs to mixture then add other eggs, and enough flour to make dough easy to handle. Mix well. Put into greased bowl, grease top of dough with melted butter. When double in bulk, knead and let double again. Form rolls, put in greased pan, using melted butter on top. Let rise to double and bake at 425° 10 - 15 minutes.

Mrs. Tillie Levy

COFFEE ROLLS

2 cakes yeast
1 cup sour cream
¼ cup warm milk
4 cups flour or more
½ pound butter

¼ pound melted butter
4 tablespoons sugar
cinnamon, sugar, nuts, raisins
grated lemon rind

Dissolve yeast in milk. Cream butter with sugar. Add sour cream. Mix well. Add yeast and flour. Make a smooth dough and put in refrigerator over night. Next morning, roll out dough very thin. Brush with melted butter and spread with pecans cut up fine, raisins, cinnamon, sugar and grated lemon rind. Roll like jelly roll and cut in pieces. Bake in moderate oven until barely brown.

Can be filled with apples or dates and nuts. Can be cut in triangles and rolled into horns. Freezes well.

Mrs. Sam Werlin (Marcelle)

MUNDELBREAD

4 eggs
1 cup sugar
½ cup oil
4 cups flour

3 teaspoons baking powder
pinch salt
1 teaspoon vanilla
1½ cups chopped nuts

Beat eggs and sugar until light. Add oil, vanilla, salt and blend. Sprinkle some of flour over nuts, and add nuts, flour and baking powder to batter and blend thoroughly. Take small amounts of batter and roll into 1 inch rolls on floured board. Place on greased cookie sheet and bake in 350° oven until they begin to brown (about 20 - 25 minutes). Remove from oven and slice rolls into pieces ¼ to ½ inch thick. Spread slices on cookie sheet and return to oven until golden.

Makes about 100 pieces.   *Mrs. Jacob Siegel (Iris)*

SCHNECKEN OR PECAN ROLLS

2 cups sugar
5 whole eggs
1½ pints milk
2 cakes yeast
2 sticks butter

salt
3 pound sack of flour
cinnamon
pecans
raisins

Heat milk and butter. In large bowl put sugar, salt, and 2 cups flour. Dissolve yeast in warm water. Add milk mixture and beat; add beaten eggs and then dissolved yeast. Beat well. Add enough flour (with pinch of salt) to handle—knead—place to rise. Next morning, roll out dough. Cover with melted butter, sugar, cinnamon, nuts and raisins. Roll up as a log, cut, dip each piece in sugar and cinnamon mixed with a little flour. Place in muffin tins that have melted butter and pecans in bottom of each one. Let rise. Bake at 350° for 45 minutes.

Mrs. Alex Wolff, Sr. (Irene)

PEABODY VANILLA MUFFINS

4 cups flour
2 eggs
4 ounces melted butter (1 stick)
2 cups sugar

2 cups milk
1 tablespoon baking powder
2 tablespoons vanilla

Beat sugar, and eggs together, add milk, baking powder, butter, vanilla, and flour. Mix thoroughly. Bake in hot greased muffin pans about 20 - 30 minutes.

Mrs. Henry Wexner, Sr. (Helen)

POPOVERS

2 eggs
1 cup milk
1 cup sifted flour

½ teaspoon salt
2 teaspoons melted butter

Grease muffin pan well with butter and heat in oven until sizzling hot. Beat eggs well, add milk and beat again with rotary beater. Sift in flour and salt, then melted butter, beating well. Put in hot pan ½ full and place in 450° oven for 30 minutes. Reduce heat to 350° for another 10 - 15 minutes.

Makes 9.

Mrs. Henry Wexner, Sr. (Helen)

SOUP'S ON!

SOUPS, GARNISHES

and CASSEROLES

B. Sartorius

SENATE RESTAURANT BEAN SOUP
Yankee Bean Soup

1½ pounds navy beans
water
3 quarts cold water
3 large yellow onions, chopped
butter

6 stems parsley
2 carrots, chopped
1 pound smoked ham
salt and pepper

Put 1½ pounds of navy beans in large bowl. Add water to cover. Let soak overnight. Drain the beans and run under hot water. Put beans in large soup pot and add 3 quarts cold water. Add onions which have been browned slightly in butter, parsley, carrots, and ham. Cover and cook slowly for about 3 hours or until reduced by half and the beans are done. Remove 2 cups of beans and puree. Return to soup with 2 cups water. Season with salt and pepper to taste.

Serves 8.

Mrs. Norman Schneidler (Barbara)

FANNIE'S BORSHT

3 pounds short ribs or lean
   meat, cut up
3 quarts water
2 cups large dried lima beans
1 medium head of cabbage,
   cut up

2 cans tomato soup
1 small piece citric acid
¾ cup sugar
1 can beets, diced
2 large potatoes, diced

Bring meat and beans to a boil in the water. Skim the top. Boil about 1¼ hours. Add cabbage, tomato soup, citric acid, and sugar. Boil another ½ hour. Add drained beets and potatoes. Continue to boil till potatoes are soft, about 20 minutes.

Ample for a meal, and even better on second day.

Serves 8.

Mrs. Leon Weiner (Sandra)

RED BORSHT (Cold)

1 can shoestring or diced beets
2 eggs, beaten
2 cans water
juice of 2 lemons

1 tablespoon sugar
salt and pepper
sour cream

Bring beets and water just to a boil. Cool slightly. Add eggs, salt, pepper, lemon juice, and sugar gradually. Cool. Serve with sour cream.

Serves 4.   *Mrs. Joseph Engler*
                                  Sent by *Mrs. Joseph Cherner*

CLAM CHOWDER

1 package frozen peas and
    carrots
2 cans frozen cream of potato
    soup

1 can cream of celery soup
1 quart of milk
2 cans minced clams

Add the milk to the first three ingredients. When hot, add the minced clams and cook 5 minutes.

Serves 10.   *Mrs. Milton Gugenheim (Aileen)*

CRAB BISQUE

¼ cup green onions, finely
    chopped
½ stick butter
¼ cup flour
dash pepper
½ teaspoon seasoned salt

¼ teaspoon monosodium
    glutamate
½ pound white lump crab meat
1 quart milk
¼ cup (or less) sherrry

Saute onions in butter until wilted. Add flour, then milk and seasonings. Stir in crabmeat, then sherry and let simmer (not boil) a few minutes. Serve in bouillon cups or small bowls.

Serves 6 - 8.   *Mrs. Si Sartorius (Bunny)*

GAZPACHO ANDALUZ

(A specialty of Laurent's Restaurant in New York)

1 clove garlic, mashed
5 very ripe tomatoes, peeled
  and chopped
1 medium onion, chopped
parsley, chopped fine
3 tablespoons olive oil
1 cup beef stock or consomme
¼ teaspoon paprika

2 tablespoons vinegar
Accompaniments:
cucumbers, chopped
tomatoes, peeled and chopped
green pepper, chopped
onion, chopped
croutons

Put garlic and onion in blender and liquefy. Add all other ingredients and run blender for 2 or 3 minutes. Season to taste with salt and pepper. Chill. Serve in chilled plates. Pass accompaniments at table.

Serves 6.   *Mrs. Joel Levy (Tudy)*

GAZPACHO SOUP (Spanish)

2 onions, chopped
4 green peppers, chopped
1 cucumber, peeled and
  chopped
1½ cups tomato juice
½ teaspoon pepper
⅔ cup olive oil

2 cloves garlic, minced
5 large tomatoes, chopped
3 tablespoons celery, chopped
2 teaspoons salt
2 teaspoons paprika
⅓ cup vinegar

Put onions, garlic, peppers, tomatoes in electric blender. Add salt, pepper, and paprika; slowly add olive oil and continue to beat. Add vinegar and more seasoning if desired (a dash of tabasco is good). Chill at least 2 hours in a wooden or glass bowl (never metal). Before serving add cucumbers and celery. May be garnished with croutons or minced parsley. Serve very cold.

Serves 6 - 8.   *Mrs. A. A. Kaufman (Jean)*

GUMBO — LOUISIANA STYLE

6 slices bacon, crumbled
1½ pounds okra
4 medium onions, chopped fine
6 pods garlic
1 cup flour
1 green bell pepper, chopped
   fine
1 #2 can of tomatoes
2 cans tomato paste

3 quarts chicken stock
salt and pepper to taste
1 tablespoon Worcestershire
   sauce
2 pounds crabmeat or 2 pounds
   shrimp or 1 pound of each
1 pound crab fingers (optional)
1 tablespoon gumbo file
1 cup hot water

Cook 6 slices of bacon until crisp, and remove from grease. Fry in bacon grease until not stringy—1½ pounds of okra. In another skillet, saute onions, garlic (mashed through garlic press), 1 green bell pepper. Add to cooked okra. Brown 1 cup of flour in a dry skillet. Add to above mixture, and cook for a few minutes until well mixed and brown, stirring constantly. Add tomatoes, tomato paste, chicken stock, salt and pepper to taste, and Worcestershire sauce.

Add seafood. (You may substitute chicken for seafood.)

Let cook until thick. Just before serving, heat to a boil, cut off fire and add 1 tablespoon gumbo file that has been dissolved in 1 cup hot water. Serve with rice.

Serves 8.   *Mickey and Jules Breitenbach*

HEARTY MEATBALL SOUP

1½ pounds ground chuck
3 tablespoons butter or
   margarine
1 can (1 pound, 12 ounce)
   tomatoes, undrained
2 cans (10½ ounce size)
   consomme, undiluted
1 can (1¾ ounce) dry onion
   soup mix
½ cup celery tops, chopped

4 pared carrots, sliced ¼ inch
   thick
½ cup parsley, chopped
1 bay leaf
½ teaspoon dried oregano
   leaves
½ teaspoon dried basil leaves
½ teaspoon salt
10 peppercorns

With hands, lightly shape ground chuck into 1 inch balls. In hot butter in 6 quart saucepan, saute meatballs turning until browned all over. Drain off fat. Add rest of ingredients and 1 cup water; bring just to boiling. Reduce heat, and simmer, covered, 45 minutes, stirring occasionally to break up tomatoes. Serve very hot.

Serves 8. *Mrs. Robert Harris (Anne)*

NEVER FAIL MATZO BALLS

1 cup water
5 tablespoons chicken fat or 2 tablespoons chicken fat and 3 tablespoons salad oil

1 cup matzo meal
3 whole eggs, beaten
black pepper, salt
parsley, chopped

Boil water with fat or oil. When it comes to a boil stir in matzo meal. Let cook until it leaves side of pan. Take pan from fire and let cool.

Add eggs, salt, pepper, and parsley. Form into balls.

Let water come to boil, add salt and matzo balls. When it comes to boil again, turn to low and simmer, covered, for 20 minutes.

Serves 6. *Mrs. Edward Levy (Edna)*

MATZO BALLS

6 tea matzos
3 tablespoons chicken fat
5 scallions or green onions, cut fine

4 eggs, well beaten
salt, pepper and nutmeg
fresh parsley, chopped

Soak matzos in water for a long time. Squeeze and drain. Melt chicken fat in skillet. Simmer onions in chicken fat. Add drained matzos and fry until dry over slow heat. When cool, add eggs, matzos, salt, pepper and dash of nutmeg. Add a generous amount of fresh parsley. If necessary, add matzo meal to make stiff enough to roll. Boil in soup or in salted water.

Makes 50 very small balls. *Mrs. Abe Zuber (Stella)*

SHERRIED LOBSTER BISQUE

2 cans condensed cream of
    mushroom soup, undiluted
2 cans condensed tomato soup,
    undiluted

⅔ cup dry sherry
1 cup light cream
2½ cup milk
1 can (5 ounces) lobster meat

In a large kettle combine soups and mix well. Stir in sherry, cream, and milk. Drain lobster, removing membrane, and add to soup. Bring just to a boiling point over medium heat, stirring occasionally. To serve, pour soup into a warm tureen or soup cups and garnish with finely minced green onion.

Serves 8.   *Mrs. Jerry Bass (Phyllis)*

HANNAH WESTHEIMER'S GUMBO

(Originated in Breaux Bridge, Louisiana)

1 cup all purpose flour
1 cup meat drippings
3 large onions, chopped
3 cloves garlic, chopped
3 pounds okra (thinly sliced
    crossways)

1 bell pepper, finely chopped
black pepper, white pepper,
    and salt to taste
3 pounds crab meat or 2 dozen
    whole crabs
3 pounds cleaned shrimp

Brown flour in ¾ cup drippings, stirring constantly. Add 1 quart water and set aside.

Saute onions, garlic, okra, and pepper in rest of drippings.

Add to thickened flour gravy. Stir until smooth. Add another quart of water, salt, and pepper. Boil very slowly about 20 minutes. Add crab meat and shrimp. Add enough water to insure 15 bowls. Boil slowly another 20 minutes. Serve over hot rice. Serve garlic bread and green salad with gumbo.

Serves 15.   *Mrs. I. B. Westheimer (Fannie)*

SPLIT PEA SOUP

3 quarts cold liquid*
1½ cups dried split peas
1 large onion, chopped fine
2 tablespoons flour

salt and pepper to taste
2 tablespoons bacon fat
2 tablespoons celery, chopped
4-5 weiners

Wash and soak peas overnight in water to cover. Drain and boil slowly for 3 hours in meat stock in a covered pot, adding celery, salt, and pepper while cooking. Put through a fine sieve and return to fire and continue cooking until liquid is reduced to about 3 pints. Heat bacon fat in skillet, add onions and flour and brown. Mix a few spoons of soup with onions and add mixture to soup pot. Cook 10 minutes and add cut up weiners and cook 20 minutes more.

*Liquid from cooking a smoked tongue or corned beef. (You may use plain water, but the meat stock improves the flavor.)

Mrs. Albert A. Kaufman (Jean)

SKILLET BEEF SUPREME

½ pound lean beef (sirloin tip preferred)
2 tablespoons salad oil
1 onion
1 green pepper, sliced
1 cup celery, sliced
1 cup fresh green beans, cut up

4 teaspoons cornstarch
1 tablespoon soy sauce
¾ cup water
4 ounce can sliced mushrooms
salt
pimentos
1 can water chestnuts (optional)

Slice beef ¼ inch thick. Cut into strips. Brown in salad oil. Add onion, green pepper, celery and green beans; cook 3 to 5 minutes. Combine cornstarch with soy sauce and water. Add to skillet. Stir in sliced mushrooms; cook about 5 minutes. Stir and cook until liquid is clear and shiny and beans are tender. Salt, then garnish with pimentos. Serve with rice. Water chestnuts may also be added.

Serves 4.

Mrs. Sydney Cohen (Harriet)

CHOW MEIN

2 pounds of beef, preferably
    sirloin tip
2 beef bouillon cubes
3 onions, sliced thin
1 rib celery, diced
1 can bean sprouts
1 can bamboo shoots

1 can water chestnuts
1 can sliced mushrooms
3 tablespoons cornstarch
2 tablespoons bead molasses
rice or Chinese noodles
soy sauce

Cut beef into ¼ inch strips; cook gently with enough water to cover. Add bouillon cubes. Lay onions and celery over meat, cover and let cook until vegetables are fairly soft. Drain bean sprouts, bamboo shoots, chestnuts, and mushrooms. To one cup juice from meat mixture, add cornstarch and molasses. Blend until smooth, add to meat mixture with soy sauce to taste. Heat slowly. Serve over rice or Chinese noodles.

Serves 4 - 6.

Mrs. Joel Levy (Tudy)

"DULUTH, MINNESOTA BEANS AND BEEF"

2 pounds round steak or 3
    pounds lean short ribs or
    combination of both to
    equal 5 pounds

1 pound large lima beans
2 cans tomato soup
1 cup brown sugar
½ cup maple syrup

Soak beans 1 hour in cold water with 1 teaspoon salt. Place in large pan with cut up meat. Cover with twice amount of water as meat. Salt. Skim. Keep boiling until water has boiled down covering meat and beans. (About 1½ hours.) Place in roaster, add brown sugar and tomato soup. Bake at 350° at least an hour. Remove cover the last ½ hour, and sprinkle maple syrup over it.

Mrs. Leon Weiner (Sandra)

LASAGNA

2 tablespoons salad oil
1½ pounds ground beef
2 cloves garlic, crushed
1 - 6 ounce can tomato paste
1 - 8 ounce can tomato sauce
1 #2 can tomatoes
1½ teaspoon salt
½ teaspoon oregano

¼ teaspoon coarse ground black
  pepper
8 ounce package broad lasagna
  noodles
1 pound mozzarella cheese,
  sliced
1 pint small curd cottage cheese
grated parmesan cheese

Heat oil in skillet, add ground meat and garlic. Brown slowly; add tomato paste, tomato sauce, tomatoes, salt, pepper and oregano. Cover and simmer one hour. Cook noodles in boiling salted water, drain and rinse. Fill a casserole with alternate layers of noodles, mozzarella cheese, cottage cheese, meat sauce and parmesan cheese, ending with layer of sauce and cheese. Bake in 375° oven 45 minutes.

Mrs. Joe Corman (Rika)

SPAGHETTI CHILI

1 pound ground round steak
2 cans tomatoes, regular size
3 medium onions
¼ cup salad oil

4 tablespoons chili powder
1 teaspoon salt
1 package spaghetti
1 can red kidney beans

Chop onion and saute in oil. Add a little water to steam. Add meat, and brown. Add other ingredients and cook. When done, add cooked spaghetti and kidney beans.

Mrs. Morris Kline (Lillian)

SPANISH DELIGHT

1 large onion
1 large green pepper
4-5 tablespoons bacon drippings
1½ pounds ground beef
1 #303 can of tomatoes

1 pound can of cream style corn
1 tablespoon chili powder
1 box medium width noodles
yellow cheese, grated

Chop onion and green pepper. Saute in bacon drippings until tender. Add ground meat and sear. Then add tomatoes, cream style corn, and chili powder. When this mixture has cooked thoroughly add the noodles Cook till noodles are tender, then put in a baking dish, and top with grated cheese. Run in oven until the cheese melts.

Mrs. Evelyn Landa Nixon

ARROZ CON POLLO

½ pound rice
3 pound chicken, cut in pieces
1 pint of chicken stock
3 tablespoons dry wine
1 tablespoon tomato paste
1 onion, diced
1 green pepper, diced

2 cloves garlic, minced
½ teaspoon saffron
salt and pepper
1 can sweet red pepper
1 can of peas (petit pois)
1 can artichoke hearts

Fry chicken slightly in hot oil; add onion, green pepper and garlic. Fry a little longer and add salt, pepper and stock. Let it come to a rapid boil. Add wine and rice, stir; cover and cook for a half hour on slow fire. Decorate casserole with sweet red peppers, peas and artichoke hearts.

Serves 4.

Mrs. Harold Tanenbaum (Dorothea)

CHICKEN BREASTS CASSEROLE

6 chicken breasts
1 teaspoon salt
½ teaspoon paprika
¼ teaspoon pepper
6 tablespoons butter
¼ pound fresh mushrooms

12-15 ounce can artichoke
hearts
2 tablespoons flour
⅔ cup consomme
3 tablespoons sherry

Season the chicken breasts in the salt, pepper, and paprika. Then brown in 3 tablespoons of butter and place in casserole. Saute the remaining butter with the fresh mushrooms, until they are tender. Sprinkle the flour over the mushrooms and blend in the consomme and sherry. Allow to simmer lightly for 3 minutes. Arrange artichoke hearts around chicken in casserole and cover with the mushroom consomme sauce. Bake at 375° for 45 minutes.

Serves 6.

Mrs. John Landa (Nancy)

CHICKEN SPAGHETTI

3½ to 4 pound hen
1 onion, chopped
4 ribs of celery, chopped
3 cans tomato sauce
1 can tomato soup
1 can water

salt and pepper
pinch of red pepper
mushrooms (optional)
parmesan cheese
2 boxes spaghetti

Boil hen in seasoned water until tender. Remove hen and save soup stock to boil the spaghetti. When cool, remove chicken from bones. Saute onions and celery in large skillet in either shortening or margarine until tender. Add tomato sauce, soup and water. Season with salt, pepper, and red pepper. Cook slowly, stirring often. Add mushrooms, if desired. Cook 2 boxes spaghetti in chicken soup about 15 minutes. Pour off liquid. Spread spaghetti in baking pan, mix chicken, sauce and spaghetti. Serve hot with parmesan cheese.

Mrs. Lasker Meyer (Lucille)

CHICKEN, ARTICHOKE & MUSHROOM CASSEROLE

1 - 3 pound frying chicken
1½ teaspoons salt
¼ teaspoon pepper
½ teaspoon paprika
6 tablespoons butter

1 can (303) artichoke hearts
2 tablespoons flour
1⅓ cup chicken broth
4 tablespoons sherry
¼ teaspoon dried rosemary

Cut chicken into serving pieces and sprinkle with salt, pepper and paprika. Brown in 4 tablespoons of the butter and remove to casserole. Add the remaining 2 tablespoons butter to the drippings and saute sliced mushrooms in this. Arrange artichoke hearts in between the chicken pieces. Sprinkle flour over the mushrooms and stir in chicken broth, sherry, and rosemary. Cook for a few minutes, then pour over the chicken and artichokes. *Cover* and bake in 375° oven for 40 minutes or until tender. Serve with mixed green salad and rice. Gravy is very rich.

Serves 4.   *Mrs. Sidney L. Mayer (Betty)*

CORN AND TAMALE CASSEROLE

1 cup celery, chopped fine
1 large onion, chopped fine
1 large red-green pepper, chopped fine
4 cups cream sauce, medium thickness, with ½ stick butter added

½ stick butter or margarine
3 eggs
4 large cans whole kernel corn, drained
4 cans chicken tamales, cut into ½ inch pieces
grated American cheese

Put ½ stick butter in large skillet and cook vegetables until tender, but not brown. Make cream sauce and let cool. Beat in 3 whole eggs, then add cooked vegetables. Stir well; add salt and pepper. Butter casserole and make alternate layers of corn, tamales, sauce, ending with cheese. Sprinkle with paprika. Bake in 350° oven for 20 - 25 minutes.

Serves 10 - 12.   *Mrs. Sam Weiss (Lillian)*

GREEN ENCHILADAS

onions (chopped)
green chiles (cut fine)
tomatoes (cut in small pieces)
butter

grated American cheese
tortillas
sour cream

Stew onions, chiles and tomatoes together. Dip one tortilla at a time into hot butter for a second. In buttered casserole make a layer of tortillas, cheese, sauce—then repeat, ending with tortillas. Spread top with sour cream, run into oven and serve.

Quantities to be used vary according to individual tastes.

Mrs. Henry Desenberg (Helen)

SHRIMP AND ARTICHOKE CASSEROLE

(President and Mrs. Kennedy enjoyed this recipe in
Mr. Adlai Stevenson's home.)

1 #2 can artichoke hearts
¾ pound cooked shrimp (1 pound fresh shrimp)
1½ cup cream sauce (I use can cream of celery or mushroom soup
¼ pound fresh mushrooms, sliced (canned may be used)

2 tablespoons butter
1 tablespoon Worcestershire sauce
¼ cup dry sherry wine
¼ cup grated parmesan cheese
salt, pepper, dash paprika
chopped parsley

Drain artichoke hearts; arrange in buttered baking dish. Place cooked shrimp over them. Saute mushrooms in butter for 6 minutes and add to baking dish. Add Worcestershire sauce and sherry to cream sauce and pour over contents of baking dish. Sprinkle top with parmesan cheese and paprika and bake 20 minutes in 375° oven. Garnish with chopped parsley.

Mrs. Benjamin Cohen (Saralee)

49

CRAB MEAT NOODLES SUPREME

1 pound lump crab meat
2 cups ketchup
½ cup water
1 small onion, chopped
2 ribs celery

2 tablespoons butter
½ pound American cheese,
   grated
1 small package noodles

Saute onions and celery until tender (not brown). Add ketchup, water, salt, and pepper to taste. Cook 20 minutes, add crab meat, and cook 5 more minutes. In buttered casserole, put layer of cooked noodles, crab meat sauce, and add half of grated cheese. Repeat, ending with remaining cheese. Bake in 350° oven until it bubbles, or approximately 30 minutes.

Mrs. M. A. Frimel (Helen)

PAELLA

¼ cup olive oil
2 cloves garlic, crushed
2 large onions, minced
2 cups raw rice
6 cups chicken stock
dash of red pepper
dash of black pepper
¼ teaspoon thyme
¼ teaspoon rosemary

½ teaspoon saffron
salt
2 cups mixed shellfish (shrimp,
   clams, etc.)
2 cups mixed vegetables
8 or more pieces fried chicken
1 cup butter, melted
parsley

Heat oil in deep skillet. Add garlic, onion, rice and pepper. Stir constantly until rice browns. Add chicken stock, thyme, rosemary, saffron, and salt. Cover. When it boils turn to low heat and simmer, stirring occasionally. Remove lid, and cook until all liquid is absorbed. Add shellfish, mixed vegetables, chicken and parsley to rice mixture. Pour over butter. Bake at 400° for 20 minutes.

Mrs. Joseph Engler (Rikey)

FISH AND VEGETABLE CASSEROLE

(*A meal in One*)

1½ pound red fish, cut into 4 or 5 steaks (save head)
2 medium potatoes, pared and sliced thin
1 medium onion, peeled and sliced thin
3 of 4 ribs celery, cut in pieces

1 medium green pepper, cored and sliced thin
2 large carrots, sliced thin
1 package frozen green peas
flour, salt, pepper, ketchup, butter

Grease a deep oblong casserole, flour slightly. Place a layer of vegetables, sprinkle with a little flour, salt and pepper to taste, dot with butter and dribble ketchup over all. Repeat with a second layer. Season fish with salt and pepper, place on top of vegetables, fish-like fashion (head first, etc.) put small pats of butter on top of fish. Cover tightly with foil and bake in 350° oven for 2 hours.

Serves 4 - 5. *Mrs. I. S. Knobler (Goldie)*

SHRIMP ASPARAGUS CASSEROLE

3 pounds shrimp, cooked and cleaned
3 cans green asparagus tips
3 hard boiled eggs, chopped
1 cup blanched almonds, chopped

6 ribs celery, chopped
mayonnaise, enough to make smooth consistency
cracker crumbs
2 small cans pimento, chopped

Split shrimp in half. Mix with eggs, celery, pimento, almonds and mayonnaise. Carefully fold in asparagus tips. Place in greased casserole; top with cracker crumbs. Bake 30 minutes in 350° oven.
From the Island of Hawaii—a real gourmet dish.

Serves 12. *Mrs. Lew Harris (Henny)*

SHRIMP AND NOODLE CASSEROLE

4 ribs celery, chopped
2 onions, chopped
1 large green pepper, chopped
1 can tomato soup
1 can mushroom soup

⅓ cup water
2 pounds yellow cheese, grated
3 packages narrow noodles
3 pounds shrimp (boiled)

Saute celery, onions and pepper. Mix soups together with water and add to sauteed vegetables. Cook a few minutes. Put into greased casserole in following order: layer of noodles, cheese, shrimp, then soup mixture, and alternate, ending with cheese on top. Sprinkle with paprika and bake until cheese is melted.

Serves 12. *Mrs. Sam Weiss (Lil)*

SALADS, MOLDS and DRESSINGS

E. Sartorius

ASPARAGUS SALAD, MARINATED

1-2 cans asparagus (judge 3-4 per serving. Many people like the larger sizes of asparagus)

Marinade:
1 cup salad oil
1 cup vinegar
1½ teaspoons salt
½ teaspoon pepper

1 small clove garlic
Dressing:
finely chopped raw celery
tomatoes
green pepper
chopped carrots
½ bottle chili sauce

Marinate asparagus overnight. Drain about 2 hours before serving. Use the marinade as the base for the salad dressing, adding the finely chopped vegetables (blender may be used) and the chili sauce. To assemble, put the asparagus on a romaine lettuce leaf. Spoon the salad dressing over the asparagus in a banding effect. Place a band of finely chopped hard boiled egg over the dressing.

Mrs. Milton Gugenheim (Aileen)

GREEN BEAN SALAD, MARINATED

50 calories per serving
3 tablespoons cider vinegar
2 tablespoons water
1½ tablespoons salad oil
1 teaspoon salt

⅛ teaspoon pepper
1 teaspoon chopped dill or parsley
3 cups cooked green beans

Combine the vinegar, water, oil, salt and pepper, and dill or parsley. Pour over the beans. Let marinate one hour. Serve the marinated beans cold on crisp lettuce leaves.

Serves 6.

Mrs. Edward J. Levy (Edna)

THREE BEAN SALAD

1 can green beans
1 can wax beans
1 can red kidney beans
2 thinly sliced onions
1 green pepper sliced
½ cup finely chopped parsley

Bring to boil:
¾ cup sugar
⅔ cup white vinegar
⅓ cup salad oil
1 teaspoon salt
½ teaspoon black pepper

Pour boiling liquids over drained bean mixture. Place in ice box for at least two or three days, mixing daily.

Serves 10 - 12. *Mrs. Charles Strauss (Florence)*

DILLED GREEN BEAN SALAD

2 packages frozen whole green beans
2 thinly sliced cucumbers
Dressing:
1 cup sour cream

1½ tablespoons powdered dill
1½ teaspoons salt
1 tablespoon lemon juice
(refrigerate)

Cook green beans. Drain and add cucumbers. Refrigerate.
Before serving, add dressing and toss well.

Serves 8. *Mrs. L. M. Landa, Jr. (Lois)*

CABBAGE SALAD

2 quarts of cabbage—shredded
  (1 large head)
3 thinly sliced onions
3 thinly sliced green peppers
Bring to boil:
1 pint vinegar

2 cups of sugar (make it rather
  sweet—but less if desired)
1 tablespoon salt
¾ tablespoon celery seed
¾ tablespoon mustard seed
¾ tablespoon turmeric

Pour this boiling mixture over the cabbage and let set 24 hours.

Mrs. S. W. Asher (Bettye)

COLE SLAW — I

1 medium head cabbage,
   shredded
1 tomato diced
2 or 3 shallots, chopped
1 cup mayonnaise or salad
   dressing

1½ teaspoons salt
⅛ teaspoon pepper
⅛ teaspoon paprika
1 teaspoon sugar
2 tablespoons milk
2 tablespoons vinegar

Let stand at least 2 hours.

Serves 10.   *Mrs. Thomas Freundlich, Jr. (Cecile)*

COLE SLAW — II

¼ cup horseradish (white)
½ cup mayonnaise
2 tablespoons red wine vinegar

1 tablespoon sugar
1 medium cabbage (red)

Mix dressing together and mix with shredded red cabbage.

Serves 4 - 6.   *Mrs. Sam Shapiro (Ruth)*

EGG CHOW CHOW RING

11 hard boiled eggs
⅔ cup chopped ripe olives
⅔ cup chopped chow chow
1 cup mayonnaise
1 bottle tiny pearl onions

1 tablespoon gelatin
½ cup water
1 teaspoon Worcestershire
   sauce
salt, pepper, paprika to taste

Rice eggs. Soak gelatin in ½ cup water, dissolve completely over hot water. Mix eggs, olives, chow chow, and onions with mayonnaise. Add gelatin and seasoning. Pour into oiled ring mold and let chill. When turned out can be garnished with any vegetables. Serve with 1000 island dressing. Fill with chicken salad for luncheon main course.

Mrs. Sam Weiss (Lil)

GUACAMOLE

4 avocados
2 lemons
½ small grated onion (onion
juice)

Lawry's salt
cayenne pepper
pinch salt

Mash avocados and add other ingredients.

Mrs. Joel Brochstein (Lynn)

UNUSUAL GUACAMOLE SALAD

*I suppose we all like a different salad every once in a while, and this
fills the bill beautifully.*

6 avocados
1½ teaspoons salt
2 teaspoons vinegar
2 tablespoons mayonnaise
1 teaspoon salad oil

6 drops tabasco
½ small hot pepper minced
½ cup finely chopped raw
tomato
¼ cup finely chopped onion

Dice peeled avocados into small pieces and place in bowl. Add remaining ingredients, and stir until well mixed. Add more salt and tabasco as needed. Serve on lettuce leaf. Prepare ahead.

Serves 6 - 8.

Mrs. Milton Gugenheim (Aileen)

MELITZANOSALATA (Eggplant Salad)

This is good served with drinks or with dinner.

1 large eggplant
¼ cup olive oil
salt and pepper
1 clove garlic
1 tomato diced

2 tablespoons minced parsley
1 tablespoon grated onion
1 teaspoon oregano
2 tablespoons white wine
vinegar

Bake eggplant in moderate oven (350° F.) 1 hour. Cool, peel and dice. Put olive oil, salt and pepper in bowl and rub with cut clove or garlic. Discard garlic. Combine eggplant, tomato, parsley, onion and oregano in the bowl. Pour vinegar over and mix thoroughly. Chill.

Serves 4.

Mrs. Joe Corman (Rika)

DUTCH POTATO SALAD

5 pounds large new potatoes
3 bunches of green onions
(stripped down to tender
part)
½ cup chopped parsley

Hot French Dressing:
white vinegar
salad oil
white pepper
sugar   salt

Bessie says this French dressing must be made "to taste," but should be on the tart side.

Boil potatoes in jackets in salt water. Do not overcook. Peel and slice while warm. Add onions, pour boiling dressing over potatoes and onions. Add parsley, and salt if needed. Do not refrigerate the day used. Prepare early in the morning to use that evening.

Serves 8.

Mrs. Walter Pye, Sr. (Bessie)

RELISH RING

1½ teaspoons unflavored
gelatin
2¼ cups tomato juice

½ teaspoon salt
1 jar India relish, drained

Soften gelatin in ¼ cup cold tomato juice. Heat 2 cups of tomato juice; add salt. Add cold gelatin mixture and chill. When semi-firm, fold in drained relish. Pour into ring mold. Chill.

Serves 8 - 10 (as a side dish).

Mrs. Robert Rothschild (Anita)

TOMATO ASPIC SALAD

1 package lemon gelatin
Cover and simmer 10 minutes:
2 cups tomato juice
1 tablespoon vinegar
1 tablespoon chopped onion

1 teaspoon or more whole
   cloves
½ teaspoon salt
few celery leaves

Add gelatin while hot. Strain. Pour into individual molds. May add artichoke hearts, chopped celery, and sliced ripe olives.

Mrs. M. M. Macow (Shirley)

ANCHOVY-TOMATO SALAD

Per person:
1 thick slice of tomato
cream cheese to cover tomato
anchovy paste

Holland rusk
1 leaf Boston red tip
1000 island dressing
rolled whole anchovies

Soften cream cheese and add small amount of anchovy paste to taste. Place lettuce leaf on plate; add Holland rusk, tomato, frosted with cream cheese mixture. Cover with any desired dressing. Top with an anchovy.

Mrs. L. M. Landa, Jr. (Lois)

VEGETABLE ASPIC

1 cup cold water (juice of
   vegetables)
3 tablespoons gelatin
2 cups boiling water
½ cup wine vinegar

1 teaspoon salt
juice of lemon
paprika
½ cup sugar
2 cans mixed vegetables

Dissolve gelatin in cold water. Add to boiling water. Add remaining ingredients except vegetables. Let thicken until soupy, then add vegetables.

Mrs. Sydney Cohen (Harriet)

TOMATO ASPIC

1 large can tomato juice (1 pint,
   2 ounces)
1 onion
2 stalks celery
salt-pepper
juice of 1 lemon
Worcestershire
1 package unflavored gelatin

1 small can petits pois peas
1 small can diced beets (pickled
   day before)
1 small can asparagus points
1 small jar pimento olives
   (sliced)
¼ cup green pepper (diced
   very small)

Boil and strain first 6 ingredients. Do this immediately. Dissolve 1 envelope of unflavored gelatin in a little water. Add to hot juice. Set aside.

Rub mold with a little oil. Add vegetables that have been mixed. Cover with tomato juice. Put in refrigerator to congeal. Serve with homemade mayonnaise.

Mrs. Abe Zuber (Stella)

BING CHERRY SALAD RING

1 #2½ can bing cherries
   (pitted)
2 cups orange juice
1½ cups sherry

1 cup sugar
3 tablespoons gelatin
nut meats

Mix juice from cherries with 1½ cups orange juice, wine and sugar; bring to boil. Soak gelatin in remaining orange juice. Dissolve in hot fruit syrup. When mixture begins to set, put into mold or individual molds, placing cherries which have been stuffed with nut meats in the jelly. Serve with fruit mayonnaise.

Serves 12.

Mrs. Sidney L. Mayer (Betty)

61

APRICOT MOLD

2 packages orange-flavored
gelatin
1 can apricots

1½ cups of apricot syrup
½ pint whipping cream
2 cups boiling water

Dissolve gelatin in boiling water. Add syrup and cool until partially jelled. Beat with rotary beater until stiff enough to hold its shape. Force apricots through sieve (or mash in blender). Add apricots and whipped cream to gelatin mixture. Pour into spring form.

Serves 10 - 12. *Mrs. Henry Meyer (Ruth)*

BLUEBERRY MOLD (Large) — I

4 packages lemon-flavored
gelatin
4 cups pineapple juice

2 large cans blueberries
1 pint whipping cream
2 ripe bananas, mashed

Drain juice from blueberries; heat with pineapple juice. Dissolve gelatin in hot juices. Refrigerate until soupy. Fold in bananas, blueberries and whipped cream and turn into mold.

Mrs. Sydney Cohen (Harriet)

BLUEBERRY MOLD — II

1 package pineapple or lemon
flavored gelatin
1 package raspberry flavored
gelatin

2 cups boiling water
¾ pint sour cream
1 #2 can blueberry pie filling

Add one cup boiling water to pineapple or lemon gelatin. When cool, add sour cream and pour into mold to harden. Pour another cup of boiling water into raspberry gelatin. When cool, mix in blueberry pie filling. Pour on top of other mold when set.

Serves 6 to 8. *Mrs. Bob Bernstein (Tiby)*

CHERRY MOLD

1 large cherry-flavored gelatin
1 large can and 1 small can
  black bing cherries
1 large can and 1 small can
  crushed pineapple

2 - 12-ounce bottles of cola
  beverage
1 cup chopped nuts
4 tablespoons mayonnaise
1 - 8-ounce pkg. cream cheese

Boil 1 cup cola; add to the gelatin. Mix well until the gelatin is dissolved. Add rest of cola and the juice of the cherries. Chill until almost set. Add drained cherries, pineapple, nuts, mayonnaise, and cream cheese which has been grated in slivers while cold. Mix thoroughly and refrigerate until firm.

Serves 18 to 20. *Mrs. Leon Phillips (Jerry)*

FRESH CITRUS MOLD

4 navel oranges
2 cups fresh orange juice
juice of ½ lemon
2 envelopes unflavored gelatin

½ cup sugar
2 grapefruits
¼ cup confectioners' sugar

Grate rind from 1 of the oranges and set the 4 whole oranges aside to use later on. Prepare orange juice from additional oranges. Strain and measure correct amount; squeeze juice from ½ lemon and strain. Pour ½ cup of the orange juice into a bowl and sprinkle gelatin over the top to soften. After 5 minutes stir in 1½ cups boiling water and sugar. Stir until dissolved. Add orange rind, remaining 1½ cups orange juice, and lemon juice. Pour into a serving bowl and chill until firm. While the jelly chills, peel skin and white membrane from the 4 whole oranges and the grapefruits with a sharp knife. Section the fruit in neat pieces, discarding seeds and fibers between the sections. Mix orange and grapefruit pieces with confectioners' sugar very gently and chill. Unmold and arrange the fruit sections around mold.

A teaspoon of Cointreau or Curacao over each serving of citrus sections is delicious.

Serves 6 - 8. *Mrs. Irving Gold (Selma)*

CREAMY FRUIT SALAD

1 #2 can fruit cocktail
1 envelope unflavored gelatin
1 tablespoon lemon juice
1 - 3 ounce package cream
   cheese

¼ cup mayonnaise
dash salt
⅔ cup whipping cream
½ cup sugar
½ cup chopped nuts

Drain the fruit cocktail. Soak gelatin in lemon juice and dissolve over hot water. Blend cream cheese with mayonnaise and salt. Stir in gelatin. Whip cream until stiff, adding sugar gradually during last stages of beating. Fold in cheese mixture, nuts and fruit. Pour into refrigerator tray that has been lined with wax paper. Freeze until firm.

Serves 8 - 10.   *Mrs. Saul Friedman (Elaine)*

CRANBERRY SALAD MOLD

2 packages cherry-flavored
   gelatin
1 cup hot water
1 cup sugar
1 tablespoon lemon juice
1 cup pineapple juice

1 cup drained crushed
   pineapple
1 cup chopped celery
½ cup chopped nuts
1 orange, ground
1 cup raw ground cranberries

Dissolve gelatin in hot water. Add sugar, lemon juice, and pineapple juice. Chill till nearly set. Add remaining ingredients. Chill until firm.

Yield: Large ring mold.   *Mrs. A. Scharff (Ida)*

CRANBERRY MARLOWE

1 cup cranberry sauce
⅔ cup boiling water

15 marshmallows
½ pint whipping cream

Dissolve marshmallows in boiling water. Add cranberry sauce. Beat with rotary beater, and chill. When mixture begins to thicken, fold in cream which has been whipped. Freeze in refrigerator trays or mold.

Serves 6.   *Mrs. Henry Meyer (Ruth)*

FROZEN FRUIT DELIGHT

1 tablespoon butter
1 tablespoon flour
1 cup pineapple juice
2 tablespoons lemon juice
1 tablespoon sugar
few grains salt
1 egg, beaten
½ cup miniature marshmallows

1 cup sour cream
½ cup nuts, chopped
1 cup pineapple, canned, cut
   into small pieces
1 cup bananas, sliced
1 cup strawberries, fresh, finely
   cut

Melt butter. Add flour and mix well. Add pineapple juice slowly and cook over medium heat, stirring until sauce is thickened and smooth. Add lemon juice, sugar, and salt. Pour small amount of hot mixture over beaten egg and blend. Return mixture to heat and cook about 3 minutes longer, stirring constantly. Remove from heat; add marshmallows and stir until dissolved. Cool. Fold in sour cream, nuts, and fruit. Pour into refrigerator tray and freeze. Let stand at room temperature a short time before serving.

Serves 6 - 8.   *Mrs. Melvin Maltz (Phyllis)*

FRUIT SALAD

1 cup Mandarin orange
   sections, drained
1-2 cups pineapple chunks
   drained
½ cup maraschino cherries,

   drained
1 cup nuts (optional)
1 cup miniature marshmallows
1 cup shredded coconut
1 cup sour cream

Mix all ingredients together. Chill for several hours.

Serves 8 - 10.   *Mrs. Cecil Weil (Maxine)*

MOLDED SALAD SUPREME

1 package lemon-flavored
   gelatin
1 cup fruit juice (drained from
   canned fruit)
1 cup salad marshmallows
juice from 1 lemon

1 pint whipping cream
1 can bing cherries (pitted)
1 can crushed pineapple
1 cut up banana
½ cup chopped nuts

Dissolve jello in heated fruit juice. *Let cool.* Add lemon juice, marsh-mallows, nuts, fruit. Fold in whipped cream. Place in ice-box till jelled. *This recipe is in 1-1-1 amounts. For a larger mold, increase the number of boxes of gelatin and cans of fruit accordingly. However, for the largest size mold which might call for as many as three cans of each size fruit, do not use more than two bananas and not more than two pints of whipping cream at the most. Be sure the jello is cool before the whipping cream is added or it will curdle.

Mrs. Ben Battelstein (Virginia)

LIME-ALMOND SALAD

1 package lime-flavored gelatin
¾ cup hot water
1 cup mashed cottage cheese
½ cup blanched almonds
   ground
1 ground cucumber

1 ground onion
1 tablespoon lemon juice
1 cup mayonnaise
Dressing:
1 cup of whipped cream folded
   into 1 cup of salad dressing

Dissolve flavored gelatin in water. When thick, add other ingredients. Chill in mold.

Mrs. Rebecca Miller

GREEN GAGE PLUM MOLD

1 large can green gage plums
1 - 8-ounce pkg. cream cheese

1 large package lime-flavored
   gelatin

Strain plums well, pit, and puree. Use juice from plums to form cold liquid (2 cups), plus 2 cups hot water, less 2 tablespoons. You may layer the mold with plums and jello. (Blend cream cheese with small amount of jello). Layer cream cheese (in a long pan). Blend all together for individual molds.

Mrs. Joe Corman (Rika)

PINEAPPLE-CARROT MOLD

1 package lime-flavored gelatin
1 package lemon-flavored
  gelatin

1 small can crushed pineapple
4 small carrots grated

Use juice of pineapple instead of cold water called for on package and make gelatin as otherwise directed. Add other ingredients. Mold in individual custard cups or in a large mold. Before unmolding, place cups of mold in warm water and loosen with knife.

10 mold capacity.   *Mrs. Charles Newman (Diane)*

HOT FRUIT COMPOTE

1 pound can of peach halves
1 pound can of apricot halves
1 pound can of pear halves
1 pound can of pineapple
1 pound can of pitted black
  bing cherries

bananas
butter
brown sugar
slivered almonds (blanched)
¼ cup sherry wine
almond macaroons, crushed

Drain fruit for several hours, and place on paper towel to dry. Cut fruit in chunks. Butter large casserole and arrange fruit in mixed layers, using dab of butter between each layer. Sprinkle generously with brown sugar and slivered almonds until casserole is filled. Add wine. Cover with macaroons. Bake in preheated 350° oven for 20 minutes. Serve warm. To be served with fowl or meat.

Serves 10.   *Mrs. Charles Strauss (Florence)*

GOLDEN FRUIT COMPOTE

6 large juicy apples
1 box dried apricots
3 firm bananas, sliced
2 small cans undiluted orange
    juice
4 tablespoons apricot brandy

¼ cup cinnamon sugar
1 can drained pineapple chunks
2 tablespoons grated lemon
    rind
1 can drained white cherries

Peel and slice apples. Sprinkle with cinnamon sugar. Add all ingredients except cherries. Blend carefully. Turn into heavy casserole and bake at 300° for 45 to 60 minutes. Add drained cherries and blend with wooden spoon. Heat for 10 minutes. Should be thick, golden, and free from liquid. Good with meat or fowl.

Mrs. David Toomin (Shirley)

HAWAIIAN CHICKEN SALAD

6 breasts of chicken
lemon juice
1 cup celery, chopped

pineapple tidbits, drained
salad dressing or mayonnaise

Cook chicken and cut up. Sprinkle with lemon juice, add celery and pineapple tidbits. Add enough salad dressing or mayonnaise to hold together.

Mrs. Ted McWharf (Wanda)

MOLDED CHICKEN SALAD

1 envelope unflavored gelatin
½ cup cold water
1 can cream of chicken soup
¼ teaspoon tabasco
2 tablespoons lemon juice

½ cup cold water
¼ cup mayonnaise
1 can (5 ounce) boned chicken
1 small can water chestnuts,
    drained and chopped

Mix gelatin in ½ cup cold water to soften. Place over boiling water and stir until dissolved. Blend ½ cup water with soup. Stir in dissolved gelatin, tabasco, lemon juice, and mayonnaise. Chill mixture until consistency of unbeaten egg whites. Fold in remaining ingredients. Turn into mold and chill until firm.

3 cup mold capacity.   *Mrs. Arthur Simon, Jr.* (*Wilma*)

WEST INDIES SALAD

1 pound fresh lump crab meat
1 medium onion, chopped fine
4 ounces salad oil

3 ounces cider vinegar
4 ounces ice water
salt and pepper

Spread one half of onions in bottom of large mixing bowl. Separate crab meat lumps and place on top of onions, then spread balance of onions on top of this. Salt and pepper to taste (cracked pepper may be used). Add first the oil, then the vinegar and lastly the ice water. Cover and place in refrigerator to marinate from 2 - 12 hours. When ready to serve, toss lightly.
Can be used as first course or served on tomatoes or green lettuce as a salad.

Serves 6 - 8.   *Mrs. Arthur Glassman* (*Lenore*)

TOMATO & SHRIMP ASPIC

1 can tomato soup
1 can water
1 package lemon-flavored
    gelatin
1 envelope unflavored gelatin

¾ pound cooked shrimp
chopped celery and green
    pepper
1 tablespoon pickle relish
1 teaspoon vinegar

Heat tomato soup and water. Dissolve gelatin in mixture. Cool. Add remaining ingredients and place in mold.

Serves 6.   *Mrs. Leonard Lipson* (*Betty*)

MOLDED SHRIMP SALAD

1 can tomato soup
2 or 3 packages cream cheese
1 cup mayonnaise
1 envelope gelatin (unflavored)
1 tablespoon lemon juice
¼ cup water
1 pound cooked broken shrimp

1 cup celery
½ cup of chopped or grated
  onion
¼ cup chopped green pepper or
  pimento
dash of tabasco

Heat tomato soup and add cream cheese which has been softened. Soak gelatin in water and add to tomato soup mixture in double boiler. When cool, add mayonnaise and the rest of ingredients. Pour into mold.

Mrs. Albert Meyerson (Bertha)

SHRIMP AND CUCUMBER RING

1½ pounds cooked shrimp
1 package lemon-flavored
  gelatin
½ cup hot water
1 teaspoon salt
1 teaspoon dry mustard

1 tablespoon horseradish
1 tablespoon minced onion
2 cups cucumbers peeled and
  diced
¼ cup minced parsley
1 cup sour cream

Dissolve gelatin in hot water, slowly. Stir in next four ingredients and chill until slightly thickened. Stir in shrimp, cucumbers, parsley, and sour cream. Pour into 1½ quart ring mold and chill until firm. Optional: top each serving with mayonnaise and capers.

Mrs. David Hymans (Bernice)

TUNA SALAD

1½ heads of lettuce
2 cans tuna (chunk)
2 cucumbers
2 teaspoons chopped onion
2 teaspoons lemon juice

2 teaspoons sugar
salt
½ can chow mein noodles
½ pint sour cream
½ cup salad dressing

Break up lettuce, add cucumbers cut in half slices. Mix rest of ingredients except noodles. Add ½ can noodles just before serving. Toss together.

Serves 6 - 8.   *Mrs. Abner Burg (Bess)*

CAVIAR SALAD DRESSING FOR LETTUCE

juice of 3 lemons   1 can caviar
½ pint salad oil   chili sauce to taste
4 hard boiled eggs, riced   salt and pepper

Squeeze juice of lemons into bowl. Add salad oil, eggs, caviar and chili sauce to taste. Season with salt and pepper if desired. Let stand awhile before using.

Mrs. H. Levy (Elsie)

BUD BIGELOW'S REMOULADE SAUCE

Measure the following into a   2 teaspoons red apple cider
mixing bowl: vinegar
2½ tablespoons yellow mustard   ¼ teaspoon salt
2½ tablespoons Creole mustard   ⅛ teaspoon pepper
2 teaspoons bottled horseradish   ½ teaspoon chili powder

Mix well, add one pint mayonnaise and stir until well blended.

For measuring purposes, chop coarsely the following:

½ cup celery   1 small clove garlic
⅓ cup green onions (tops and   ½ hard boiled egg
    all)

Put vegetables through meat grinder using coarse blade. Do not use blender. Combine chopped vegetables and seasoned mayonnaise and mix well by hand. Store in covered jars in refrigerator.

Yield—1½ pints.

GREEN GODDESS DRESSING

Place in blender:
½ cup sour cream
1 cup mayonnaise
3 tablespoons tarragon vinegar
1 tablespoon lemon juice

3 tablespoons chopped fresh
  chives
⅓ cup parsley
½ clove garlic
1 can flat anchovy filets, drained

Blend until ingredients form a smooth mixture or until they are only coarsely chopped, according to one's taste. Is best used in salads made of romaine lettuce or spooned over a wedge of iceberg lettuce.

Yield—1 pint.   *Mrs. Gerald Katz (Doris)*

ITALIAN SALAD DRESSING

1 quart salad oil
6 eggs
1 - 6-ounce bottle Worcestershire sauce
1 - 14-ounce bottle ketchup
½ pint hot mustard

1 teaspoon tabasco sauce
6 anchovy filets
4 pods garlic (chopped fine)
2 tablespoons salt
1 tablespoon black pepper
1 cup wine vinegar

Place salad oil in deep bowl and add eggs, whipping until thick. Add remainder of ingredients and whip about 5 minutes. Put in bottles and store in refrigerator.

When ready to use for 2 to 20 add the following to two cups of above mixture. (If desired.)

1 clove garlic
1 filet anchovy
¼ hard boiled egg
salt and pepper
¼ cup olive oil

1 teaspoon Worcestershire
  sauce
1 tablespoon wine vinegar
juice of ½ lemon

Mash garlic, anchovies and egg in bowl; add rest of ingredients and blend. Add 2 cups of Italian salad dressing and blend again.

Serve on green salad, shrimp, etc.

Mrs. Sam Friedman (Dorothy)

BLEU CHEESE DRESSING

2 tablespoons chopped green
   onion
1 clove garlic, crushed
¼ cup parsley
1 cup mayonnaise

½ cup sour cream
1 tablespoon lemon juice
¼ cup vinegar
2 ounces crumbled bleu cheese
salt and pepper

Combine all ingredients in blender until well mixed. Chill.

Mrs. Norman Schneidler (Barbara)

ROQUEFORT CHEESE DRESSING

This one is an original. My mother experimented, tested, and produced this simple salad dressing.

3 - 3 ounce pkgs. cream cheese
¼ cup milk
¼ cup salad oil
¼ cup vinegar
1½ teaspoons sugar
1 teaspoon salt

dash pepper
juice of ½ lemon
3 ounces crumbled Roquefort
   cheese
1 cup sour cream

Place all ingredients except the Roquefort cheese and sour cream in blender, or mix by hand. Blend well. Then add the other two ingredients and stir well.

Mrs. Milton Gugenheim (Aileen)

THOUSAND ISLAND DRESSING

1 cup stuffed olives, chopped
1 cup celery, chopped
2 hard boiled eggs, chopped

1 bottle of chili sauce
⅔ cup mayonnaise

Combine all ingredients.

Yield—about 1 pint.

Mrs. Cecil Weil (Maxine)

FRENCH DRESSING

1 cup salad oil
½ cup vinegar
juice of ½ lemon
1 teaspoon dry mustard
½ cup tomato ketchup

1 teaspoon salt
sugar to taste (I put one
  tablespoon)
juice of onion
clove of garlic on toothpick

Place ingredients in jar and shake well.

Mrs. Morris Kline (Lillian)

MAYONNAISE

1 egg
1 cup salad oil
¼ teaspoon salt

¼ teaspoon white pepper
¼ teaspoon cayenne pepper
juice of ½ lemon

Beat egg and salt lightly in blender. Slowly add ¾ cup of the oil, then pepper, then lemon juice, then remainder of oil. Taste and re-season if desired. Powdered mustard may be added. Keep refrigerated.

Mrs. Emile Kaliski (Lorraine)

GENIE HARRIS' MORTON SALAD DRESSING

2 tablespoons Durkee's dressing
½ teaspoon paprika
1 tablespoon olive oil or salad

oil
2 tablespoons sugar
½ cup vinegar

Mix all together in blender. Pour in bottle and keep refrigerated. Wonderful to serve inside avocado-half or on grapefruit and avocado sections.

Mrs. Raymond Cohen (Alyda)

POPPY SEED SALAD DRESSING

1 cup honey
1 teaspoon salt
⅔ cup vinegar
2 tablespoons prepared mustard

5 tablespoons poppy seed
2⅔ cups salad oil
small grated onion, optional

Mix all together in order listed. Blend in electric blender or mixer until oil disappears.

Mrs. M. M. Macow (Shirley)

POPPY SEED DRESSING

3 tablespoons onion juice
1½ cups sugar
2 cups oil
⅔ cup vinegar

2 teaspoons salt
2 teaspoons dry mustard
3 tablespoons poppy seeds
   (toasted in oven)

Beat in mixer until thick.

Yield—1 quart.

Mrs. Milton Gugenheim (Aileen)

BUD BIGELOW'S TARTAR SAUCE

*Measure the following into a
  mixing bowl:*
1 cup coarsely chopped green
  onions (tops and all)
½ cup coarsely chopped dill
  pickles

⅔ cup coarsely chopped parsley,
  no heavy stems
1 tablespoon capers including 1
  teaspoon juice
½ teaspoon salt
¼ teaspoon pepper

Toss in the bowl to mix, then put thru meat grinder using the coarse blade. Stir into 1 quart mayonnaise. Store in refrigerator in covered jars.

Use this thousand island dressing variation:
To two cups tartar sauce add ⅓ cup ketchup and stir until well mixed.

Yield—slightly over 1 quart.

MIKE SALVATO'S WHITE DRESSING

3 whole eggs beaten medium
   stiff
1 pint oil—which is added
   very slowly
2 ounces fresh onion juice
juice of 1 lemon

1 clove garlic chopped very fine
1 teaspoon dry mustard
dash of tabasco
salt and white pepper
¼ cup sour cream
¼ cup mayonnaise

Mix and refrigerate.

Yield—1 quart.   *Mrs. Morton Seline (Anita)*

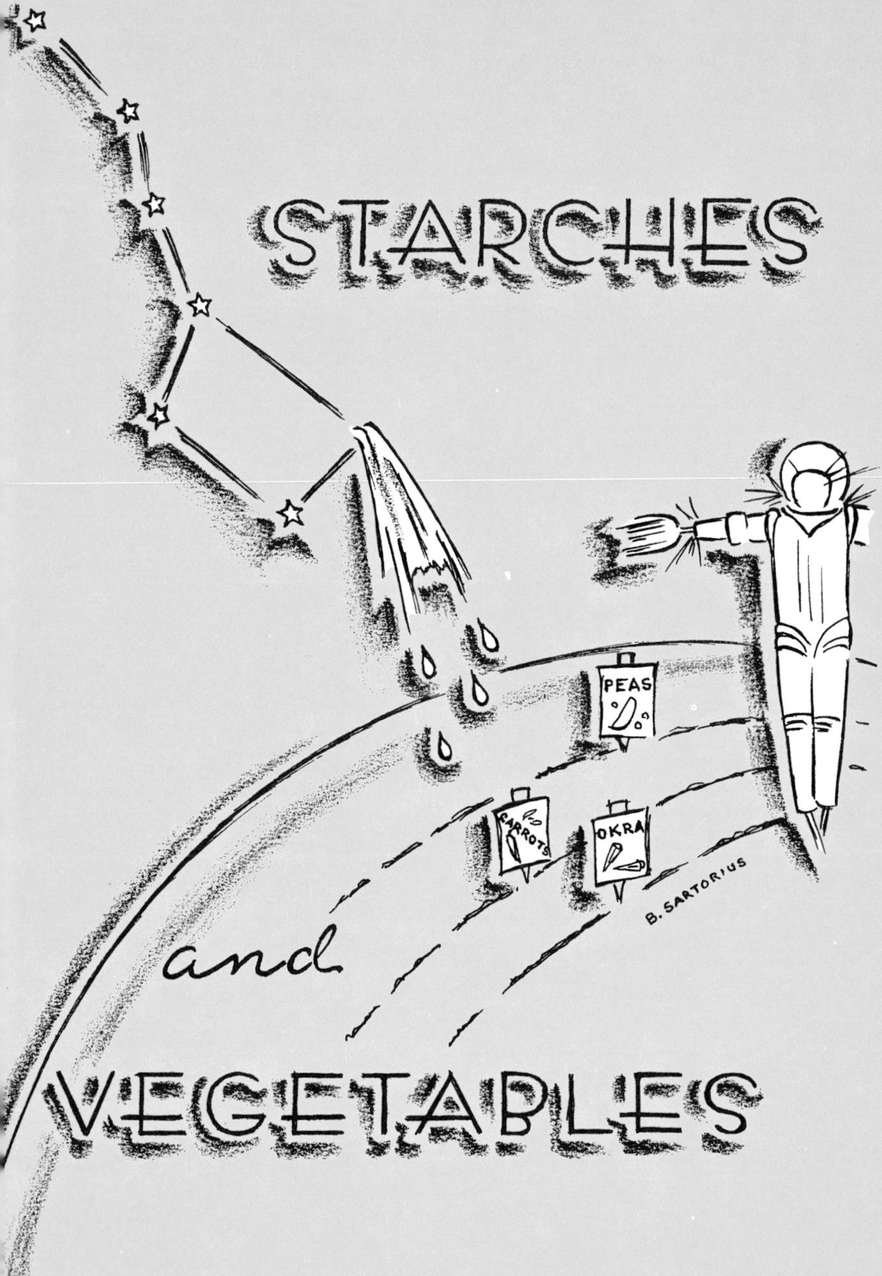
STARCHES
and
VEGETABLES
PEAS
CARROTS
OKRA
B. SARTORIUS

BAKED BARLEY

½ cup onions, chopped
6 tablespoons butter
½ cup barley

3 cups chicken broth or
consomme

Saute onions in butter until just barely soft. Add barley and brown lightly with the onions. Season to taste with salt and pepper, and put in casserole. Add 1½ cups broth. Cover casserole, and bake 30 minutes in a 350° oven. Add another 1½ cups of broth and cook until the liquid is completely absorbed.

Variations of the Baked Barley:

With Mushrooms—Add ½ pound of sliced fresh mushrooms which have been slightly sauteed in 4 tablespoons of butter. Add to barley, and place in casserole.

With Almonds—Proceed as in basic recipe and add the sliced mushrooms. After adding the liquid for the second time, sprinkle the top of the casserole with ½ cup finely chopped almonds.

With Pine Nuts and Herbs—Proceed as in basic recipe. Add ½ cup finely chopped parsley, ¼ cup chopped chives or green onions and ½ cup pine nuts. Add broth and cook as directed.

Serves 6.   *Mrs. Leonard Gold (Selma)*

DUMPLINGS

2 cups sifted flour
4 teaspoons baking powder
½ teaspoon salt

2 teaspoons butter
¾ cup milk

Sift dry ingredients together—cut in butter. Add milk. *Handle lightly* and roll on floured board. Pinch off with teaspoon, making small balls and drop in boiling liquid. Cover tightly. When liquid returns to boil lower heat and cook 15 minutes.

5 servings.   *Mrs. William Gold (Lillyan)*

CORN BREAD FISH STUFFING

½ pan cornbread, crumbled
4 slices white bread, soaked and
  squeezed dry
4 strips bacon, fried and
  crumbled
1 onion, chopped

3 ribs celery, chopped
1 green pepper, chopped
1-2 tablespoons water
1 #202 can tomatoes
worcestershire sauce
1 egg

To the grease from fried bacon add the cut up vegetables, fry until golden brown. Add water and cook an additional few minutes. Add cornbread and white bread to above ingredients. Add ½ of the tomatoes, salt, pepper, and worcestershire sauce. Mix well and add bacon. Add the egg to bind. Fill fish and place remaining dressing in pan. Pour rest of tomatoes over dressing and around fish. Bake in covered roasting pan for about 15 minutes then uncover for another 15 minutes or until done in a 425° oven.

Mrs. Milton Gugenheim (Aileen)

NOODLE RING I

2 large packages of broad
  noodles
3 cups sugar
1 cup raisins

½ cup flour
4 eggs
1 tablespoon vanilla
½ stick butter

Cook noodles and rinse once. Beat the eggs with 2 cups of the sugar, add flour, vanilla, and fold in raisins. Combine this mixture with the noodles, and bake in a 375° oven for 1½ hours in a greased ring mold. Turn out on rimmed pan. Melt together 1 cup of sugar and ½ stick of butter and let them caramelize. Pour over noodle ring. Heat for ½ hour before serving.

Serves 8.

Mrs. Melvin Maltz (Phyllis)

NOODLE RING II

½ pound medium noodles
1½ cups evaporated milk
1 onion, chopped
1 green pepper, chopped
1 pimento, chopped

2 tablespoons butter
1 cup grated yellow cheese
¾ teaspoon salt
¼ teaspoon pepper
2 eggs, well beaten

Cook noodles. Melt butter in a skillet and add the onion and green pepper, cooking until soft. Add noodles and remaining ingredients. Transfer to a buttered ring mold. Bake at 350° for 30 to 45 minutes.

Serves 8.   *Mrs. Gus Block (Gay)*

NOODLE PUDDING I

1 large bag broad noodles
1 pound grated sharp cheddar
    cheese
1 stick butter
salt

cinnamon
sugar
4 apples, grated
2 cups seedless raisins
1 pint creamed cottage cheese

Boil noodles until tender. Rinse well in hot water and drain. In large mixing bowl add cheese, butter and hot noodles and stir until butter and cheese are melted. Add salt, cinnamon, and sugar to taste; add grated apples, raisins and cottage cheese. Place the noodle mixture into either individual pyrex custard cups or a large casserole which has been buttered and sprinkled with cinnamon and sugar before filling. Bake at 375° for thirty minutes. Individual cups may be turned out easily and should be served immediately.

Serves 12.   *Mrs. A. A. Kaufman (Jean)*

NOODLE PUDDING II

1 - 8-ounce package fine
noodles
½ pound cream cheese
¼ pound butter (less if desired)
½ package onion soup —
optional

3 tablespoons sugar
1 cup of milk
4 eggs
crushed corn flakes to cover top
cinnamon to taste

Boil noodles in salted water according to directions on package. Drain. While still hot, add cream cheese, butter and the onion soup. When the ingredients have been well blended, add the sugar, milk and eggs. Pour into a greased 8 by 12 inch baking dish. Cover with the corn flakes combined with cinnamon. Bake at 350° for 1 hour.

Serves 6 to 8.   *Mrs. Jake B. Sampson (Pauline)*

FARFEL CASSEROLE

1 box barley egg noodles
(untoasted)
2 small onions, chopped

1 stick butter
2 tablespoons chicken fat
1 can chopped mushroom pieces

Boil egg noodles as directed on box. Saute onions in butter and chicken fat. Add chopped mushrooms and pour over blanched farfel, mixing well. Place into a greased casserole and bake at 325° for twenty-five minutes.

Serves 8.   *Mrs. L. M. Landa, Jr. (Lois)*

CONFETTI ALMOND RICE

3 tablespoons butter
⅛ teaspoon curry powder
1 tablespoon onion, finely
chopped
½ cup slivered toasted almonds

1 teaspoon salt
few grains black pepper
¼ cup parsley, finely chopped
1 can pimiento, finely chopped
3 cups cooked rice

Melt butter, add curry powder and onion. Cook until onion is soft. Add almonds, salt, pepper, parsley and pimiento. Toss lightly into hot and fluffy rice. Serve while hot.

Serves 6.   *Mrs. S. W. Asher (Bettye)*

RICE CONSOMME

1 small onion, chopped
1 cup rice
1 cup canned consomme
½ stick butter
small can water chestnuts

4 ounce can mushrooms
black pepper
small amount of celery, cut fine
1 teaspoon beef extract

Melt butter in skillet. Add onion, celery, and rice. (Do not wash or cook rice.) After it has browned, add mushrooms with juice, consomme undiluted and can of water chestnuts, beef extract and black pepper. Cover and cook until done. (Season with black pepper and 1 teaspoon beef extract to taste.) This may be put in a casserole.

Serves 6.   *Mrs. Joel Brochstein (Lynn)*

OYSTER RICE DRESSING

1½ cups cooked rice
½ green pepper, chopped
1 onion, chopped
2 stalks celery, chopped
2 pods garlic, minced

1 pint oysters, chopped
chicken stock
1 stick margarine (½ cup)
salt, pepper and Accent to taste

Saute green pepper, onion, celery and garlic in skillet with a stick of margarine. Fold in cooked rice and raw oysters. Add chicken stock to moisten slightly, and season with salt, pepper and Accent to taste. Bake at 350° for twenty minutes. (Chicken livers may be substituted for oysters.)

Serves 6 to 8.   *Mrs. Abe Rubenstein (Ethlyn)*

RICE DRESSING

1 cup rice, uncooked
2 tablespoons shortening
1 to 2 onions, chopped
2 stalks celery, chopped
1 green pepper, chopped
1 large clove garlic, crushed
2 teaspoons worcestershire

dash of red pepper
2 hard boiled eggs, finely
  chopped
salt and pepper to taste
broth or butter to moisten
turkey giblets, cooked and
  cut up

Cook 1 cup of rice according to directions on box. In a skillet melt shortening and add the onions, celery, green pepper and garlic. Cook only until soft and clear, not brown. Stir in worcestershire sauce and add salt, pepper and a little red pepper to taste. Add giblets, rice, and eggs and mix well. Add either broth or butter to moisten. When serving as a side dish add finely chopped green onions and top with minced parsley. This can be made ahead of time and heated in the oven before serving.

Serves 8.   *Mrs. M. G. Gugenheim, Jr. (Aileen)*

SHRIMP FRIED RICE

4½ cups water
3 cups raw white rice
3 eggs
¾ cup salad oil
soy sauce

salt
pepper
shallots, chopped
2 pounds shrimp, cooked

Boil water, add rice, cook till all water is absorbed and rice is cooked. In heavy iron skillet, heat oil. Scramble the eggs lightly, add rice, seasonings. Color with soy sauce to taste. Add onions and shrimp. Cook slowly. Must be prepared shortly before serving.

Serves 8 - 10.   *Mrs. Ben Krandel (Sylvia)*

MEXICAN RICE

2 tablespoons fat
1 cup rice
1 small onion, minced
1 green pepper, chopped

2 teaspoons salt
2 teaspoons chili powder
1 cup tomato juice
2 cups water

Wash rice well and dry. Brown rice in fat until golden color. Add onion and green pepper, salt, chili powder, tomatoes, and water. Mix well. Cover, cook about 30 minutes.

Mrs. Morris Kline (Lillian)

RICE PILAF

1 stick margarine or butter
3 cups minute rice
1 medium onion, chopped

1 pound fresh or canned mushrooms, sauteed in butter
3 cans beef consomme

Brown onions and rice in butter. Cook onions only until clear. Add no seasoning. Consomme contains all that is needed. Place rice mixture in a casserole and add two cans of the consomme. Put uncovered into oven at 325° for about two hours. Add third can of soup as needed for more moisture. This does well in a ring mold.

Mrs. Richard Marks (Nonie)

DUTCHESS GRUYERE POTATOES

6 or 8 potatoes, boiled
1½ cups grated Gruyere cheese
⅓ cup hot milk
4 egg yolks, beaten
salt and pepper to taste

To serve with potatoes:
sour cream
chives, chopped
caviar

Rice potatoes (5 cups). Add cheese, milk, egg yolks, salt and pepper. Beat until smooth and fluffy. On buttered baking sheet drop potato mixture, a tablespoon at a time. Broil until lightly browned.

Serves 6 to 8.

Mrs. Sam W. Levy (Grace)

POTATOES ROYAL

1 Idaho potato for each person
butter
salt
pepper

small chunks of Roquefort
   cheese
parsley flakes

Peel and slice potatoes ⅛ inch thick. Melt enough butter to cover the bottom of a large iron skillet. Line bottom of skillet with potato slices, sprinkle with salt and pepper, then add another layer of potatoes. Fry until bottom is well browned and crisp. The two layers will stick together so it is easy to flip them over. When both sides are browned, remove from skillet and place on a cookie sheet. Cover top with small chunks of Roquefort cheese. Place under broiler until cheese melts. Garnish with parsley flakes and serve immediately.

Mrs. A. A. Kaufman (Jean)

SWEET POTATO PATTIES

3-6 sweet potatoes
butter
brown sugar
salt

corn flakes, crushed
miniature marshmallows
pineapple tidbits

Bake sweet potatoes until done. Peel and force through 'Foley food mill or equivalent. Add generous amount of butter. Add brown sugar and salt to taste. Let cool—until workable—a few hours or next day. Crush corn flakes until reasonably fine. Put in a bowl or on wax paper. To a tablespoon of potato mixture, press a marshmallow and one pineapple tidbit into center. Drop gently from spoon into corn flake crumbs, and cover with flakes. Flatten slightly. Bake in a 325-350° oven about 30 minutes. May be made ahead and frozen.

Mrs. Milton Gugenheim (Aileen)

SWEET POTATO SOUFFLE

2 sweet potatoes, boiled
3 eggs, lightly beaten
1 stick butter, melted
½ cup sugar

½ to ¾ cup milk
1 teaspoon baking powder
2½ tablespoons flour
marshmallows to cover top

Mash potatoes, add all ingredients except marshmallows and put in casserole. Bake about a half hour at 350°, placing marshmallows on top for last fifteen minutes of baking time.

Serves 6.

Mrs. Si Sartorius (Bunny)

ARTICHOKE HEARTS WITH SAUCE

1 box frozen artichoke hearts
butter
1 cup salad dressing
several spoons of prepared

mustard
2 coarsely chopped hard cooked eggs
chopped black olives to taste

Cook artichokes according to directions. Drain well. Pour butter over artichokes and keep warm until serving time. Combine when ready to serve with following sauce: Fold together salad dressing and prepared mustard. Add chopped eggs and olives. Keep hot over boiling water. At serving time mix with artichoke hearts and butter.

Serves 4.

Mrs. A. F. Miller (Flora)

VEGETABLE CASSEROLE

2 small cans tiny green peas
1 large can asparagus, cut in pieces

1 large can button mushrooms
1 can cream of mushroom soup
grated sharp cheese

Alternate vegetables and soup, in layers, in a buttered casserole. Top with grated sharp cheese. Bake in moderate oven until heated.

Mrs. A. F. Miller (Flora)

ASPARAGUS ALMONDINE

2 - 303 cans green asparagus
   spears, drained
1 can cream of mushroom soup
½ cup liquid drained from
   asparagus
½ teaspoon salt

¼ teaspoon pepper
1 cup American cheese, grated
1 cup bread crumbs
4 tablespoons butter
½ cup blanched almonds

Lay asparagus in oblong casserole. Pour over asparagus mushroom soup mixed with liquid, salt, and pepper. Sprinkle with grated cheese. Melt butter, add bread crumbs, and sprinkle over grated cheese. Dot with whole almonds. Bake 45 minutes in a 300° oven.

Serves 8.   *Mrs. Al Crystal (Sara)*

BROCCOLI MOLD

2 packages chopped frozen
   broccoli
1 can mushroom soup
6 eggs
salt and pepper

1 cup mayonnaise
1 tablespoon grated onion
* 1 package frozen spinach may
   be added if desired

Preheat oven to 350°. Cook and drain broccoli. Beat eggs, add mayonnaise and soup. Add cooled, drained broccoli. Season and pour into 9 inch buttered ring mold. Place in pan of boiling water and bake for 45 minutes.

Mrs. Jake Siegal (Iris)

BROCCOLI SOUFFLE

2 packages of frozen chopped
   broccoli
medium cream sauce

2 eggs, separated
bread crumbs
parmesan cheese

Cook broccoli as directed. Drain very well. Make cream sauce using rich milk. When cream sauce is thickened, remove from heat and add yolks of 2 eggs stirring well. Combine sauce and cooked broccoli. Beat 2 egg whites until stiff and fold into broccoli mixture. Place in greased casserole and top with bread crumbs and parmesan cheese. Bake in 350° oven until top is lightly browned.

Mrs. Gerald Katz (Doris)

SCALLOPED CABBAGE

2 cups medium white sauce
5 cups shredded raw cabbage
1 cup grated cheese

2 tablespoons fine toasted
   crumbs

Mix white sauce and cabbage in 1½ quart baking dish. Top with cheese and crumbs and bake in 400° oven for 20 minutes.

Serves 6 - 8. *Mrs. David Block (Nancy)*

SWEET AND SOUR RED CABBAGE

hard whole red cabbage
2 tablespoons bacon fat
¼ teaspoon salt
2 apples, peeled and cut into
   small pieces
2 tablespoons flour

2 tablespoons sugar
⅛ cup boiling water
½ cup vinegar
½ cup raisins
1 small box ginger snaps

Soak cabbage in cold water to cover. In same cold water, place on fire and allow to boil for 15 minutes. Remove from fire and cut into small pieces. Heat fat in iron Dutch oven. Add water, vinegar, and sugar. Add flour by making paste in a cup with some of liquid and stir in slowly until all lumps are gone. Add apples, raisins, and cabbage and finally add whole ginger snaps. Cover and steam until tender. This dish may be refrigerated and re-heated if left over. It keeps nicely for several days.

Mrs. Albert A. Kaufman (Jean)

CARROT RING

1 cup shortening	1 teaspoon baking powder
½ cup brown sugar	½ teaspoon baking soda
1 egg	½ teaspoon nutmeg
1 tablespoon water	½ teaspoon each, salt and
2 cups (packed) grated carrots	cinnamon
1½ cups cake flour	

Cream shortening and brown sugar in mixer. Add the rest of the ingredients. Place in greased tin mold and bake 1½ hours in a 325° oven.

Serves 6 - 8.   *Mrs. L. M. Landa, Jr. (Lois)*
                                                Sent by *Mrs. B. Sanford*
                                                Sioux City, Iowa

CELERY AND MUSHROOM MEDLEY

3 cups celery	black pepper
1 cup chicken broth	1 teaspoon soy sauce
3 ounce can sliced mushrooms	½ cup toasted, slivered,
4 tablespoons butter or	blanched almonds
margarine	

Cut celery into ¼ inch thick crescents. Simmer in broth until just tender, then drain. Saute mushrooms in butter. Season with a little black pepper and soy sauce and add to the cooked celery. Toss with almonds and serve hot.

                                                Mrs. Sidney Mayer (Betty)

CAULIFLOWER ELIZA

1 cauliflower	⅛ pound American cheese
butter	bread crumbs
1 cup cream of mushroom soup	paprika
2 tablespoons flour	

Break cauliflower into flowerets and cook 20 minutes in boiling salted water. Drain. Place in greased baking dish. Blend in sauce pan 1 tablespoon butter, 2 tablespoons flour, and 1 cup cream of mushroom soup. Cool until thickened. Add cheese, cut fine. Pour over cauliflower, sprinkle with bread crumbs, paprika, and dot with butter. Bake in 350° oven until brown on top—about 20 minutes.

Serves 4. *Mrs. Joel Brochstein (Lynn)*

CORN AU GRATIN

1 - 12 ounce can (whole kernel) corn
butter
salt and pepper

1 tablespoon minced onion
½ cup grated Swiss cheese
½ cup cream

Butter small baking dish. Spread drained corn over bottom of dish. Add salt, pepper, onion, half the cheese. Toss lightly with fork. Sprinkle rest of cheese over top. Pour cream over all. Dot with butter and dust with pepper. Bake twenty minutes in 350° oven.

Serves 4 to 6. *Mrs. David Dochen (Sharon)*

CORN PUDDING

1 can cream style yellow corn
1½ tablespoons flour
2 whole eggs
pinch of salt

¼ teaspoon white pepper
¼ teaspoon sugar
4 tablespoons of melted butter

Beat eggs until very fluffy. Add flour and seasonings to eggs. Then add melted butter. Add corn and beat mixture very well.

Grease pyrex custard cups well and fill with corn mixture. Place cups in baking pan filled with 2 inches of boiling water. Bake at 350° until inserted toothpick comes out clean. Invert individual casseroles on platter or dinner plates.

May also be baked in large single casserole.

Mrs. William Levy (Edna)

91

CORN SOUFFLE

2 cans creamed corn
1 large bell pepper
3 eggs
⅔ cup sugar
2 tablespoons flour

¼ teaspoon nutmeg
1 cup corn flake crumbs
1 stick butter or margarine
3 tablespoons butter or
  margarine

Melt 3 spoons of butter and mix with flour in saucepan and brown. Add corn and minced bell pepper, nutmeg, sugar. Separate eggs and beat separately—whites stiff. Add yolks to mixture and fold in whites last. Pour into well greased casserole and cover with corn flake crumbs that have been well mixed with the stick of butter. Bake in 350° oven until corn mixture is well set and top is brown and crusty.

Mrs. Ike L. Freed (Sybil)

EGGPLANT ETOUFFEE

This dish may be prepared ahead of time and heated before serving.

3 medium eggplants, (one used
  for filling)
¾ cup chopped onion
¼ cup cooking oil
1 pound raw shrimp

½ cup chopped parsley
bread crumbs
butter
salt, pepper, thyme to taste

Halve eggplants lengthwise and scoop out centers leaving shells ¼ to ½ inch thick. Set shells aside. Place eggplant in ½ cup boiling, salted water and cook until soft (about 15 or 20 minutes). Use the extra eggplant to cook with other as it makes shells a little more full and rounded on top. In sauce pan saute chopped onion in cooking oil until golden. Add shrimp (peeled and cut into small pieces). Cook until pink (about 5 minutes). Add drained eggplant, chopped parsley, salt, pepper, thyme and ½ cup bread crumbs to shrimp and onions. Mix well. Place mixture into raw shells. Cover with more bread crumbs and dot with butter. Before serving bake in moderate oven in a greased baking pan. Place a little water in pan to keep eggplant from sticking.

Mrs. Simon Frank (Hank)

BAKED EGGPLANT

2½ pounds eggplant
4-6 slices white bread
½ pound American or cheddar
   cheese
3 eggs

½ cup milk
4 slices bacon diced and fried
   crisp
salt and pepper to taste
grated parmesan cheese

Peel and dice eggplant, parboil in salted water until tender, and drain. Add bread and diced cheese, bacon, salt, pepper, milk, and stir in eggs. Mix thoroughly and pour into well greased casserole. Sprinkle generously with parmesan cheese and dot with butter. Bake in 350° oven until set and the top is brown and crusty.

Mrs. Ike L. Freed (Sybil)

EGGPLANT PARMESAN

2 large eggplants
2 packages grated Mozzarella
   cheese
2 tablespoons parmesan cheese

1 large can tomato sauce
2 eggs
2 cups milk
cracker crumbs

Pare and slice eggplant (soak in cold water). Dip into batter made of beaten eggs and milk. Dip into seasoned cracker crumbs. Fry in shortening until crisp.

Butter a baking dish and make layers of eggplant, Mozzarella cheese, and tomato sauce ending with cheese. Top with parmesan cheese and bake in a 350° oven for 45 minutes.

Serves 8.

Mrs. Frank Falkstein (Farnese)

EGGPLANT AND TOMATOES

eggplant
tomatoes
salt and pepper

grated cheese or parmesan
cheese

Peel and slice an eggplant and soak in cold, salted water for one hour. Drain. Peel and slice tomatoes. Alternate layers of eggplant and tomatoes in baking dish. Place seasoning and grated cheese or parmesan cheese between layers. Sprinkle top with bread crumbs and cheese and dot with butter. Bake in slow oven for one hour.

Serves 4.   *Mrs. Irvin Shlenker (Bertha Alyce)*

KRAUT NOODLES

½ head cabbage
3 tablespoons butter

1 large package broad noodles
salt and pepper

Chop cabbage as for slaw. Saute cabbage in butter until brown. Boil noodles in salted water, drain and add to browned cabbage. Heat thoroughly. Season with salt and pepper to taste.

Serves 6.   *Mrs. David Block (Nancy)*

ONION RINGS

slice onions thin in rings
1 cup flour
1 teaspoon baking powder

enough water to make batter
consistency of thick cream

Place onions in salted ice water for 3 hours. Remove from water and dry well. Make batter from flour, baking powder, and water. Dip onions in batter and fry in deep fat until brown and crisp.

Mrs. Saul Friedman (Elaine)

LIMA BEAN AND MUSHROOM CASSEROLE

2 cups dried lima beans
½ cup butter
½ cup flour
3 cups milk
salt and pepper

½ pound fresh mushrooms
¼ cup chopped onions
2 tablespoons butter or
  margarine
¼ cup chopped pimento

Wash lima beans and soak overnight. Drain, add boiling water, and simmer until tender. Drain again. Make a cream sauce of butter, flour, milk, and salt and pepper. Clean and slice mushrooms and saute with onions in butter or margarine. Combine all ingredients carefully and add pimento. Place in a buttered casserole and bake at 300° for 45 minutes.

Serves 12.

Mrs. DeWitt Grossman (Lois)

RATATOUILLE

2 cups ½-inch cubes yellow
  summer squash
1½ teaspoons salt
3 cloves garlic, minced
⅓ cup salad oil
2 cups ½-inch cubes peeled
  eggplant

⅓ teaspoon cumin seeds
½ teaspoon oregano
3 medium sized onions, sliced
2 green peppers cut in strips
½ teaspoon marjoram
3 medium sized tomatoes, sliced
⅓ teaspoon dill seeds

Cover bottom of greased 2½ quart casserole with squash cubes. Sprinkle with ⅓ of the salt, garlic, and oil. Add cumin seeds. Make second layer with eggplant. Sprinkle with ⅓ of the salt, garlic, and oil. Add oregano. Make third layer of onion slices, fourth layer of green pepper. Sprinkle with the remaining ⅓ of the salt, garlic, oil and marjoram. Cover casserole. Bake at 350° for 1 hour. Add layer of sliced tomatoes. Sprinkle with dill seeds. Bake, uncovered, at 350° for 15 minutes. Serve hot or cold.

Serves 6.

Mrs. Robert Harris (Anne)

ALMOND-ONION CASSEROLE

2 (15½ ounce) cans whole
  onions
1½ tablespoons butter
1½ tablespoons flour
½ cup condensed mushroom
  soup (undiluted)

½ cup shredded sharp cheddar
  cheese
½ cup toasted slivered almonds
½ teaspoon accent
¼ cup sherry

Preheat oven to 350°. Drain onions and place in buttered 1 quart casserole. Melt butter in saucepan, stir in flour, soup, cheese, ¼ cup almonds, accent, and sherry. Pour cheese mixture over onions and bake uncovered for 25 minutes. Sprinkle remaining almonds on top and return to oven for 5 more minutes.

Serves 4 - 5.

Mrs. A. D. Schwarz, Sr. (Lee)
and *Mrs. Harold Gilbert (Jeanne)*

GOURMET BAKED SPINACH

2 packages frozen chopped
  spinach
2 tablespoons minced onion
3 tablespoons flour
2 cups milk
¼ teaspoon nutmeg

3 hard-boiled eggs, finely
  chopped
salt and pepper to taste
½ cup grated American cheese
½ cup buttered crumbs
paprika

Cook spinach according to directions on the package; drain thoroughly. Cook onion in butter until transparent. Add flour and blend. Add milk. Cook and stir until smooth and thickened. Add cooked, drained spinach, nutmeg and egg; season with salt and pepper to taste. Turn into a buttered baking dish and top with mixture of cheese and crumbs. Sprinkle with paprika. Bake at 375° for twenty minutes or until lightly browned on top.

Serves 6.

Mrs. Jerry Bass (Phyllis)

SPINACH AND PEAS

1 box of frozen chopped
  spinach
1 can cream of mushroom soup

1 small can tiny green peas
grated sharp cheese

Thaw and drain spinach well. Do not cook. Fold together spinach, soup and peas. Place in buttered casserole. Top with thick layer of grated sharp cheese and bake.

Mrs. A. F. Miller (Flora)

SPINACH SOUFFLE

Mold: (Prepare first in 2 quart
  mold)
butter

grated cheese
bread crumbs or flour

The sides and bottom of mold should be buttered heavily, then coated with the cheese, bread crumbs or flour. To coat, spoon several tablespoons of the coating ingredient into bottom of buttered mold. Then, holding the mold in your hands, roll it around and around so that sides and bottom are evenly but lightly coated. Turn the mold upside down and give it a good tap to get rid of any surplus. Refrigerate mold at least 30 minutes.

3 tablespoons melted butter
3 tablespoons flour
1 cup milk
¼ teaspoon salt

4 egg yolks
1 cup chopped spinach (fresh
  preferred and cooked)
5 egg whites

Blend melted butter with flour in the top of a double boiler, stirring constantly. Add milk and continue stirring the mixture till it thickens. Season with salt. When mixture has cooled slightly, add beaten egg yolks (4), and blend well. Fold in chopped spinach, then gently fold in the beaten egg whites (5). To fold in egg whites, add about ⅓ of the stiffly beaten whites, whipping them in vigorously with a small whisk. Next scoop remaining whites on top and fold in with a flat wooden spatula. Place in the 2 quart mold and bake at 375° for 35 to 50 minutes. Serve at once.

Serves 6.

Mrs. Leonard Gold (Selma)

SPINACH BERTHA

2 packages frozen chopped
  spinach
1 cup boiling water
1 teaspoon salt
2 small finely grated onions

4 tablespoons butter
1 - 3 ounce package cream
  cheese
nutmeg
salt to taste

Place frozen spinach in boiling water. Bring rapidly to second boil, separating block with fork to hasten thawing. Cover and cook gently 4 to 6 minutes or until tender. Strain thoroughly to remove all liquid. Saute onions in butter until soft. Add spinach and mix well. Place in buttered casserole and bake in moderate oven 350°. Before serving, add one package softened cream cheese cut in small cubes. Mix thoroughly and add nutmeg and salt to taste.

Serves 6 - 8.

Mrs. Louis Leon (Bertha)

SPINACH-NOODLE RING

2 packages wide noodles (white
  or green)
2 frozen packages chopped
  spinach, well drained

1 diced onion
1 cup sour cream
¼ pound margarine
4 eggs

Cook noodles in salted water for 20 minutes. Saute onion in margarine until soft. Add beaten eggs, sour cream, cooled onions, margarine and spinach to noodles. Salt to taste and mix well. Grease 3 quart mold with butter. Place mold in pan of hot water and steam in 350° oven for 45 minutes.

Mrs. Leon Weiner (Sandra)

SQUASH CASSEROLE

2 pounds small summer yellow
  squash
2 eggs, beaten slightly
½ cup onion, cut up fine
½ cup celery, cut up fine
2 tablespoons green peppers
  cut up fine (optional)

2 slices white bread moistened
  with water
1 teaspoon salt
dash white pepper
2 tablespoons butter or
  margarine
½ cup buttered bread crumbs

Boil squash in salted water until done. Mash slightly. Saute onion, celery, and green pepper in butter or margarine until clear, not brown. Combine squash, onion, celery and green pepper. Add slightly beaten eggs and moistened bread. Season with salt and pepper. Pour mixture into well greased casserole dish. Bake in 350° oven for 1 hour. Remove from oven and top with ½ cup fine bread crumbs that have been browned in butter. Return to oven to heat crumbs. Serve immediately.

Serves 6 - 8. *Mrs. I. S. Brochstein (Mildred)*

SQUASH SOUFFLE

4 tablespoons butter
4 tablespoons flour
½ teaspoon salt
1½ cups milk
1½ pounds yellow squash

2 cups grated cheese
3 eggs, separated
pimento to decorate
butter
1 can asparagus

Cook squash and let cool. Add 1 package grated cheese to white sauce made with butter, flour, salt, and milk. Mix white sauce with squash. Add 3 egg yolks. Fold in beaten egg whites. Bake 50 minutes in 350° oven. When done, add asparagus, pimento, and grated cheese in sauce and dot generously with butter. Brown in oven 10 minutes more.

Serves 4 - 6. *Mrs. Leon Davis (Ida)*

SQUASH FRITTERS

1 cup flour
1 egg
1 level teaspoon salt
2 level teaspoons baking
  powder

2 level teaspoons sugar
pinch pepper
enough milk to make stiff
4 small squash (yellow)

Cook squash until done. Let cool. Strain all water and mix flour, milk, salt, egg, sugar, and pepper, then baking powder. Dough must be very thick. Fry at once in deep fat.

Serves 4.

Mrs. Leopold Meyer (Adeline)

TOMATO SUPREME

6-8 medium-size tomatoes
1½ packages chopped spinach
  —cooked and drained
1 cup white sauce

½ pound fresh mushrooms
butter
salt
pepper

Slice top off tomatoes and remove pulp. Place upside down to drain. Make white sauce and add to cooked spinach that has been seasoned with butter, salt, and pepper to taste. Saute mushrooms (which have been cleaned, de-stemmed, and sliced) in butter until done. Add to spinach mixture. Fill tomatoes. Place in buttered casserole and bake in 350° oven for 30 minutes or until bubbly. These can be made a day before serving and refrigerated until ready to bake.

Serves 6 - 8.

Mrs. Ronny Finger (Judy)
Sent by: *Mrs. R. R. Miller*
Phoenix, Arizona

BAKED TOMATOES

tomatoes	onion
salt	sharp grated cheese
pepper	crushed potato chips

Butter flat baking dish. Slice tomatoes in thick slices. Season with salt and pepper. Slice onion very thin and place on tomato slice. Cover with cheese and potato chips. Bake 20-30 minutes.

Mrs. David Block (Nancy)

MIXED VEGETABLE CASSEROLE

2 packages frozen mixed vegetables	⅔ cup milk
1 small onion	½ pound diced sharp cheddar cheese
2 tablespoons butter	¾ cup crushed Ritz crackers

Cook vegetables until tender, drain thoroughly. Saute onions in butter, add milk and cheese and cook until cheese melts. Place vegetables in buttered 2 quart casserole. Cover with sauce, top with crumbs, paprika, and butter. Bake in 350° oven for 25-30 minutes or until done.

Serves 8.   *Mrs. Edward J. Levy (Edna)*

ZUCCHINI CASSEROLE

2 pounds zucchini	3 eggs
1 small onion	½ cup chopped celery
chopped parsley	pinch salt

Saute onion, celery and parsley. Add zucchini sliced in thin rings. Cook with onions until soft, turning often. Beat eggs and add to mixture of onion and celery. Pour into glass baking dish. Bake 50 minutes in 325° oven. Serve hot.

Serves 6 to 8.   *Mrs. David Dochen (Sharon)*

PEANUT STUFFED EGGPLANT

1 large eggplant
1 cup plus 2 tablespoons
  ground peanuts
2 tablespoons butter

½ cup milk
½ teaspoon worcestershire
salt and pepper
1 tablespoon fine bread crumbs

Cut eggplant in half lengthwise and scoop out pulp. (Save shells.) Cook pulp in boiling salted water 5-10 minutes or until just tender; drain. Mash pulp; add 1 cup peanuts, butter, milk, seasonings, mix well. Fill shells with the eggplant mixture; sprinkle crumbs and remaining 2 tablespoons peanuts over the top. Bake in a hot oven, 400°, for 15 minutes. Serve with this sauce:

6 tablespoons butter
juice of 1½ lemons

3 tablespoons finely chopped
  parsley

Combine and serve sauce in small bowl.

Serves 4 - 6.   *Mrs. Howard Barnstone (Gertrude)*

PLANTAIN TEMPTATION

*This is a native Cuban recipe and an excellent
accompaniment to chicken.*

4 ripe plantains or bananas
4 tablespoons dry wine
½ cup sugar

2 cinnamon sticks
2 tablespoons butter

Dissolve sugar in wine and add melted butter and cinnamon. Peel plantains (or bananas) and place in baking dish. Cover with wine mixture and bake in slow oven about ½ hour, turning plantains so that they become golden brown.

Serves 4.   *Mrs. Harold Tanenbaum (Dorothea)*

CANDIED APPLES

4 Jonathan or Winesap apples
1 stick of butter

sugar

Wash apples, cut in quarters, and remove cores. Melt butter in an iron skillet, dip wet quarter of apple in sugar until coated and place cored side down in melted butter. Turn often and cook over very slow fire until apples are transparent and candied. Serve hot.

Mrs. Abe Zuber (Stella)

HOLLANDAISE SAUCE

This can be refrigerated for several weeks.
Makes about 4 cups (1 quart).

1-2 egg yolks
¾ cup cream (or half and half)
salt to taste

juice of 4 lemons (more or less can be added)
¾ pound butter

Mix egg yolks, cream, lemon juice, and salt in top of double boiler over steaming water until thick. Remove from heat—add pieces of softened butter. Beat with rotary beater until well blended. This can be reheated in double boiler or under broiler. Especially good for eggs benedict.

Mrs. Milton Scheps (Joni)

MORNAY SAUCE

¼ pound butter
½ cup flour
1½ cups turkey stock or
    substitute
1 cup coffee cream

¾ pound Velveeta—diced
2 teaspoons dry mustard
2 tablespoons worcestershire
    sauce
pinch salt

Melt butter in double boiler—add flour. Add hot turkey stock, then cream and salt. Add cheese. Make a paste of dry mustard and worcestershire and add to mixture. Stir until well blended.
Good used over turkey, ham, or vegetables, etc.

Mrs. Si Sartorius (Bunny)

103

MEAT

BEEF BOURGUIGNONNE

3 pounds beef cut in cubes
(preferably sirloin steak)
2 cups red burgundy wine
1 tablespoon flour

½ cup butter
2 cups quartered mushroom
caps
¼ cup shallots, chopped

Melt butter in casserole, add beef cubes and braise in hot oven 400°
for 20 minutes. Saute mushrooms and shallots in 2 tablespoons butter.
Stir in flour, add burgundy and mix well. Pour over beef. Cover and
return to oven for 30 minutes.

Serves 6.

Mrs. David Block (Nancy)

BEEF STROGANOFF

3½ pounds of steak (loin tip)
¼ cup flour
1 teaspoon salt
2 small onions, chopped fine
½ pound mushrooms, sliced
1 clove garlic, chopped fine

3 tablespoons salad oil
2 tablespoons flour
1 can beef bouillon
1 tablespoon Worcestershire
1 cup sour cream

Cut steak in strips ½ inch thick and about 1½ to 2 inches long. Dredge
meat in ¼ cup flour and salt. Fry onions, mushrooms, and garlic in
oil for 5 minutes. Add steak to onions and mushrooms and brown.
Remove meat, onions, garlic from pan. Mix 2 tablespoons of flour in
the pan with the drippings. Add bouillon and worcestershire. Cook
until thickened. Add sour cream and heat until gravy begins to simmer.
Add meat and vegetables (mushrooms, garlic and onions) and continue to cook until piping hot. Serve over hot cooked rice or noodles.

Serves 6.

Mrs. Sol Rubenstein (Evelyn)

BEEF TENDERLOIN WITH WILD RICE STUFFING

1 whole beef tenderloin
2 boxes wild rice stuffing
2 onions, sauteed
2 stalks celery

2 eggs, beaten
1 box fresh mushrooms or
  canned sliced mushrooms

Have butcher cut pocket lengthwise through center of beef tenderloin. Cook wild rice according to package directions. Add sauteed onions, celery and eggs. Add sauteed mushrooms. Stuff rice in beef pocket and cook remaining rice in casserole. Season meat with salt, pepper, seasoning salt and worcestershire sauce. Bake in 350° oven 15 minutes per pound of meat.

Gravy

Remove meat to serving platter and use pan in which meat was cooked to make gravy. Heat the drippings, adding 2 to 3 cups of water, 2 tablespoons cornstarch (mix well with a little water removing all lumps) and the following ingredients:

1 tablespoon Kitchen Bouquet
1 tablespoon sherry
salt and pepper to taste

fresh or canned mushrooms
1 cup seedless grapes

Heat and serve over meat and additional rice.

Mrs. Bernard Perlmutter (Adele)

TENDERLOIN DANNY

8 slices beef tender (sliced
  ¼ inch thick)
¼ pound butter

½ cup chutney, chopped
¼ cup scallions, chopped

Melt butter in frying pan. Flip steak in butter. As soon as they are cooked, place on platter in low warm oven. Saute chutney and scallions in the same butter that steaks were in. Pour over tenders.

Serves 4 - 6.

Mrs. Jerry Rubenstein (Linda)

ROLLED BEEF

1 round steak
3 slices bacon, fried and crumbled (or ⅓ canned bacon)
1 onion, chopped

1 sour pickle, chopped
salt and pepper
worcestershire sauce
ketchup

Saute the onion and spread on the flat round steak; add the pickle and bacon. Season with salt and pepper. Roll with toothpicks to hold together. Place roll in flat baking dish. Sprinkle with worcestershire sauce and a little ketchup. Bake at 350° for 2 hours or until brown and tender.

Serves 3.

Mrs. William Stern (Lucille)

BRAISED BEEF IN RED WINE

3 pounds lean beef (top round)
⅓ cup butter
4 shallots
2 cloves garlic
1 bouquet garni
salt
pepper

24 carrots (small)
1 pound mushrooms
1 pound onions (small)
1 cup beef stock
¼ cup brandy
½ cup burgundy

Cut lean top round beef into 2 inch cubes, free of fat. Roll the cubes in seasoned flour and sear them in butter over high heat until they are well browned on all sides. Drain the meat and transfer it to an oven-proof casserole. Add shallots (chopped), garlic cloves, bouquet garni, salt and pepper. Cover the casserole and cook over low heat for 1½ hours. Add carrots, mushrooms, onions, beef stock, brandy, and enough burgundy to cover. Cook uncovered until the vegetables are tender (about 1 hour), basting them frequently and adding more stock if necessary. Reheating improves the flavor. Sprinkle the casserole with chopped parsley before serving.

Serves 8 to 10.

Mrs. George W. Bailes (Jean)

BRISKET OF BEEF

1 - 5-pound brisket
1 teaspoon of salt
½ teaspoon of pepper
1 can beer
2 onions, sliced

4 ribs of celery
1 cup chili sauce
dash worcestershire sauce
garlic salt

Season brisket with salt and pepper. Put in roaster fat side up. Put onions, celery, and chili sauce over meat. Add ¼ cup of water to pan. Put in 350° oven uncovered. Baste often till brown. When meat is half done add beer and cover. Allow one hour per pound.

Mrs. Sam Levy (Janis)

SWEET AND SOUR BRISKET AND SAUERKRAUT

1 large onion, chopped fine
1 tablespoon shortening
3 pounds lean brisket

salt and pepper
water
1½ cups vinegar

Fry onion soft white in shortening. Put brisket and pepper in enough water to cover and boil until tender.

Sauce:
3 cups sugar
¾ cup flour

1½ cups vinegar
salt
3½ pounds canned sauerkraut

Caramelize sugar and flour. Add to tender brisket. Add fried onion, vinegar and salt. Cook for 30 minutes stirring often. Add sauerkraut and cook until well mixed. Serve with mashed potatoes.

This recipe came from an aunt who threw things together and they came out wonderfully. I watched and copied as she made this and it has been one of our favorite cold weather dinners.

Aunt Martha Pitluk's
Serves 6.
Mrs. Frank Falkstein (Farnese)

110

NEW ENGLAND BOILED DINNER

1 bay leaf
black pepper (peppercorn)
4 to 5 pound brisket

prepared mustard
brown sugar

Simmer, *never boil,* corned beef. Wash the piece of brisket under running water. Put in a large kettle and cover with cold water. Add bay leaf and a few whole black peppers. Bring to a boil, then simmer until tender. When done, remove meat to shallow pan, reserving liquid; spread thin coat of mustard and sprinkle with brown sugar. Bake in moderate 375° oven, 20 minutes or until nicely browned.

Vegetables:
For each serving allow:
1 potato
2 carrots

2 onions
wedge of cabbage
parsley

Cook carrots and onions ½ hour, add potatoes and cook 15 minutes longer; add cabbage and cook another 15 minutes, or until all is tender. Put meat on platter and arrange vegetables around it. Garnish with parsley. Serve with horseradish, mustard, and vinegar, or plain.

Mrs. Ross Seline (Dee)

FILET OF BEEF

5 pounds filet of beef
½ onion, grated
juice of 2 lemons

2 to 3 tablespoons worcester-
    shire sauce
salt and pepper

Marinate filet over night in above ingredients. Pour off juice before baking in 400° oven, 15 minutes per pound for rare, 20 minutes medium, 30 minutes well done.

Serves 10.

Mrs. Henry Meyer (Ruth)

SAUERBRATEN

First day:
5 to 6 pound bottom round
  roast
salt and pepper
1 clove garlic, slivered
1 onion, sliced

1 quart water
½ cup vinegar
4 peppercorns
2 slices seeded lemon
1 bay leaf
2 whole cloves

Second day:
2 onions, chopped
5 tablespoons chicken fat
flour
paprika

1 teaspoon sugar or 1 lump
2 tablespoons stewed tomatoes
1 carrot, chopped fine
sour cream

Rub meat with salt and pepper. Insert slivers of garlic into meat with knife. Put meat into bowl and cover with onion slices. Boil water and vinegar. Add peppercorns, seeded lemon, bay leaf and whole cloves. Pour hot marinade over meat. Cover bowl tightly and let stand 24 hours in refrigerator. Turn occasionally.

Next day, saute 2 onions in 2 tablespoons chicken fat. Rub roast lightly with flour. Sear in skillet in 3 tablespoons fat. Add roast to onions in casserole. Add paprika, lump sugar, stewed tomatoes, carrot, and 2 tablespoons marinade. Cover tightly and put in 325° oven for 3½ to 4 hours. Thicken gravy with sour cream when ready to serve.

Serves 10 - 12.
Mrs. Harold Hecht (Pauline)

QUICK SAUERBRATEN

1 - 4-5 pound pot roast (chuck,
  round or rump)
¼ cup vegetable oil
½ cup onion, chopped
2 tablespoons mixed pickling
  spices

2 teaspoons salt
1 cup red wine vinegar
3 cups water
½ cup brown sugar, firmly
  packed
12 gingersnaps, crumbled

Brown pot roast slowly on all sides in oil in heavy kettle or Dutch oven. Pour off excess oil. Add next 6 ingredients. Simmer 3 to 4 hours or until tender. Remove meat; keep warm. Strain liquid left in kettle; measure 4 cups. Add gingersnaps. Cook and stir until smooth and slightly thickened. If thicker gravy is desired, stir in 3 tablespoons flour blended with ⅓ cup cold water. Cook, stirring often, 5 minutes.

Serves 6.   *Mrs. Sam Shapiro (Ruth)*

CHINESE PEPPER STEAK

1 pound beef tenderloin
salt and pepper
oil
¼ teaspoon accent
⅓ cup scallions, chopped
1 clove garlic, chopped

3 green peppers
1 cup Chinese cabbage, sliced
1 cup beef stock
2 tablespoons cornstarch
2 tablespoons soy sauce
2 tablespoons water

Cut beef into narrow strips against the grain. Heat oil and fry beef until brown. Add salt and pepper, scallions, garlic, green peppers and cabbage. Cover with beef stock and simmer covered for 10 minutes. Mix corn starch, water and soy sauce. Add to mixture and cook covered on a slow heat until all the ingredients are thoroughly cooked.

Serves 3.   *Mrs. Wayne Phillips (Jacquelyne)*

FLANK STEAK

1 large flank steak
salt and pepper
½ cup worcestershire sauce
½ cup A-1 sauce

1 onion
butter
1 small can mushroom pieces
noodles

Marinate flank steak all day in salt and pepper and worcestershire sauce; cover with A-1 sauce, and onion rings. Before broiling, dot with butter and cover with mushroom pieces. Broil 20 minutes (not too close to the flame). Slice thin, diagonally across grain of meat. Serve over thin buttered noodles.

Serves 6.   *Mrs. Donald Gould (Jean)*

DUDA'S POT ROAST

4 pound pot roast
coarse ground black pepper
salt
2 medium carrots
2 pieces celery
1 onion
2 strips bacon
3 or 4 peppercorns

1 small piece lemon peel
1 bay leaf
½ teaspoon salt
1½ cups water
2 bouillon cubes
2 slices rye or pumpernickle
    bread

Season roast with mixture of pepper and salt. Cut carrots and celery in strips. Slice onion. Cut bacon in small pieces and fry in Dutch oven. Remove the bacon and brown the vegetables lightly. Remove the vegetables and brown the meat. Place the meat on top of the vegetables and season with peppercorns, lemon peel, bay leaf, and salt. Add water in which bouillon cubes have been dissolved. Cover and simmer 2½ hours or until done. Crumble bread in gravy and strain through sieve or blend. Re-heat with roast.

Mrs. Joe Corman (Ricka)

SHORT RIBS

8 - 10 short ribs
salt and pepper
paprika
2 tablespoons margarine
1 large onion, diced
2 pods of garlic, minced
4 tablespoons sugar

4 tablespoons vinegar
4 tablespoons ketchup
4 tablespoons worcestershire
    sauce
1 teaspoon mustard
1 teaspoon celery seed
½ cup water

Wipe ribs and brown lightly. Remove from skillet; salt, pepper and add paprika. Saute in margarine, onion and garlic. Add rest of ingredients and cook over low fire for 10 minutes. Pour sauce over ribs arranged in baking dish. Bake 1½ hours at 350°.

Serves 4.   *Mrs. Alan Gugenheim (Renee)*

STUFFED CABBAGE BALLS

1½ pounds lean ground chuck
2 large loose leaf cabbage heads
  (about 4 pounds)
½ cup rice (uncooked)
2 small onions, grated
1 can tomato paste
1 can tomato sauce

1 cup vinegar
⅓ cup sugar
2 tablespoons salt
½ tablespoon pepper
4 cups water
1 large tablespoon flour
1 egg

Loosen cabbage leaves and cut off hard ridge on back of leaves. Dip each leaf in and out of boiling water to soften leaf. Mix meat, 1 tablespoon salt, pepper, egg, rice and grated onion together. Brown over heat to make roux; add water, vinegar, sugar, tomato paste, tomato sauce and 1 tablespoon salt. Take small amount of meat mixture, put on cabbage leaf and roll up envelope style. Hold together with toothpick. Cut up remaining cabbage very small and put into sauce. Put rolled cabbage on top of this and cook covered about 2 hours. Before serving put in baking dish and bake 1 hour.

Makes 30 balls.   *Mrs. I. B. Maltz (Nettie)*

STUFFED CABBAGE — SWEET AND SOUR

1½ pounds chopped beef
1 head cabbage
1 onion, juice of
salt and pepper
2 cans tomato sauce

1 can water
2 lemons
½ cup sugar
½ cup rice (uncooked)

Season meat with salt and pepper, onion juice and juice of 1 lemon, rice and ¼ cup sugar. Mix well. (Blend onion and lemon juice in osterizer.) Place whole cabbage in boiling water for several minutes to soften and loosen leaves. Remove limp leaves and separate. Sauce: Boil tomato sauce, water, juice of 1 lemon and ¼ cup of sugar. Roll a portion of meat in cabbage leaf, secure leaf with toothpick, and place in sauce. Simmer gently for 2 hours; serve with sauce.

Serves 4 - 6.   *Mrs. David Dennenberg (Ruth)*

CARBONADE FLAMENDE

1 pound of beef stew meat	bay leaves
1 large onion, cut up	grated nutmeg
1 stick butter or margarine	flour or cornstarch
1 can beer	salt and pepper to taste

Salt and pepper meat and fry with onion in butter or margarine until brown. Then add beer, several bay leaves, grated nutmeg and salt. Cook stew until the meat is tender. Thicken with flour or cornstarch which has been dissolved in a little cold water. Serve separately with potatoes and vegetables.

Serves 4 - 5.

Tony Renee

GLAMOUR BURGERS

cold turkey or roast, sliced	onion, sliced
cheddar cheese, sliced	mustard
ketchup	sandwich buns

Slice bun and spread each side with mustard. Place onion, turkey or roast and cheese. Spread top with ketchup. Place on cookie sheet and broil on lower part of oven for 10 minutes.

Mrs. Lew Harris (Hennie)

CHILI

2 pounds ground chili meat (chuck preferred)	3 tablespoons chili powder (more if desired)
2 cans tomato paste	salt and pepper
6 pods garlic, diced (more if desired)	½ cup pinto beans (optional)
1 large onion, cut up	2 cups water

116

Soak pinto beans in water and cook slightly. Cook chili meat, onions and garlic slowly for 30 minutes, with no water. Add water and cook 45 minutes to 1 hour more. Add chili powder, paste, salt and pepper. Add pinto beans. Cook 30 minutes more.

Serves 12.   *Mrs. Jake B. Sampson (Pauline)*

MEAT BALLS IN GRAPE LEAVES

2 pounds ground meat	2 spoons water
2 - 3 onions, finely chopped	2 cans tomatoes (drained)
grape leaves	2 cups brown sugar
salt and pepper	1 cup white sugar
ketchup	a couple pieces of sour salt
lemon juice	2 lemons, juice of
4 - 5 large onions	

Season ground meat with 2 - 3 finely chopped onions, salt, pepper, ketchup, and lemon juice. Rinse grape leaves in cold water. Saute 4 or 5 large onions in fat with water and let simmer. When onions are soft, add tomatoes and brown sugar, white sugar, sour salt, and juice of 2 lemons. Arrange layers of meat balls (wrapped in grape leaves), cover with ketchup and alternate layers. Cook slowly 3½ to 4 hours.

Mrs. Albert Meyerson (Bertha)

EGGPLANT MEAT LOAF

1 pound hamburger	1 onion, diced
¼ pound pan sausage	1 clove garlic, chopped
1 medium size eggplant	1 teaspoon chili powder
2 eggs	salt and pepper

Crumble and brown both meats. Boil eggplant; drain, chop and mix with meats. Add other ingredients and mix well. Shape into loaf and roll in flour. Brown in fat. Bake at 350° for 45 minutes.

Serves 4 - 5.   *Mrs. Morton Seline (Anita)*

SPAGHETTI SAUCE

1 pound ground meat
1 onion, cut fine
2 cans Italian tomato paste
1 can cream of tomato soup
¾ cup coffee
1½ teaspoons sugar

1 can mushrooms
seasoning salt
garlic powder to taste
3 tablespoons butter or
    margarine

Brown onions and meat in butter or margarine. Add salt (seasoned) and garlic powder. Add other ingredients and cook until thick, over low flame. Serve over spaghetti.

This recipe can be doubled and frozen.

Serves 6.

Mrs. William Boas
Mrs. Charles Freundlich (Betty)

SPAGHETTI WITH SAUCE

2 pounds ground meat (best
    quality)
3 large onions (or more),
    chopped
3 small sections of garlic,
    chopped
2 #303 cans tomatoes

2 cans condensed tomato soup
2 tablespoons cooking oil
4 tablespoons chili powder
1 cup water
2 - 7 ounce boxes long spaghetti
salt to taste

Fry onions and garlic in oil until brown. Add meat and cook until brown. Add tomatoes, tomato soup and salt. Mix chili powder and water to taste and add to mixture. Simmer about 10 minutes. Break spaghetti and drop into salted boiling water, cooking 10 minutes. Rinse spaghetti in cold water and add to tomatoes and meat mixture. Simmer for 30 minutes.

Serves 10.

Mrs. Simon Frank (Hank)

ITALIAN MEAT BALLS

1¼ pounds ground round steak
3 pods garlic, chopped fine
1 medium onion, chopped fine
parsley, chopped
¼ cup grated parmesan cheese

3 eggs
1 teaspoon dry sweet basil
3 slices bread, soaked in milk,
    salt, pepper and olive oil

Mix all together. Shape into small balls. Brown in olive oil. Cook in your favorite tomato sauce with lid off and let simmer until done. Especially good to serve with spaghetti or any other Italian dish.

Serves 6.

Mrs. Ray Cohen (Alyda)

SKEWER DOGS

1 pound ground beef
¾ cup soft bread crumbs
¼ cup milk
2 tablespoons onions, chopped
1 egg, slightly beaten
½ teaspoon salt

dash pepper
6 frankfurters
1 cup ketchup
¼ cup butter, melted
¼ cup molasses
2 tablespoons vinegar

Combine ground beef with next 6 ingredients; mix lightly. Divide meat mixture into 6 portions. Shape meat around franks, covering completely. (Roll kabobs between waxed paper to make uniform.) Chill. Insert skewers lengthwise through frankfurters. For sauce: Combine ketchup, butter, molasses and vinegar; brush over kabobs. Broil 3 inches from heat about 15 minutes, turning as needed. Simmer sauce while kabobs are cooking; brush on kabobs just before removing from heat. Serve in toasted coney buns; pass extra sauce.

Serves 6.

Mrs. Jerry Rubenstein (Linda)

MEAT LOAF

1½ pounds ground round steak
1 egg, beaten
3 tablespoons onion, diced
½ cup moist bread
¼ cup milk

1 teaspoon dry mustard
1 teaspoon worcestershire sauce
3 tablespoons ketchup
salt and pepper

Mix all ingredients well and bake at 350° for about 1 hour.

Mrs. L. M. Landa, Jr. (Lois)
Mrs. R. R. Miller

GLAZED LAMB RIBLETS

3 to 4 pounds breast of lamb,
    cut in riblets
1 large onion, chopped
4 cups water
1 teaspoon salt
¼ teaspoon pepper

1 can (13 ounce) pineapple
    chunks
¼ cup brown sugar, firmly
    packed
½ teaspoon dry mustard
¼ cup soy sauce
¼ cup vinegar

Brown riblets in large kettle, drain off fat. Add onion, water, salt, and pepper. Heat to boiling, then simmer 1 hour or until tender.

Drain pineapple juice into small saucepan (save chunks). Add sugar, mustard, soy sauce, and vinegar. Simmer 10 minutes.

Drain ribs. (Save stock to make soup another day. Can be used for onion soup if you enjoy lamb flavor.) Arrange in single layer in large shallow pan. Brush with sauce.

Broil 5 minutes, basting once, turn ribs, add pineapple chunks; brush all with remaining sauce. Broil 5 minutes longer, or until glazed a rich brown.

Serves 4.

Mrs. Ross Seline (Dee)

CHILIDRON

4 pounds lamb (cut into pieces)
1 can tomato puree
½ cup olive oil
2 tablespoons paprika
2 green peppers, chopped
1 cup onion, chopped
3 cloves garlic, minced

2 tablespoons sour orange or
  ½ lime juice
parsley (sprig or two)
1 cup dry wine
½ cup seedless raisins
½ cup blanched almonds
½ cup olives

Brown lamb in oil. Add peppers, onion, garlic, paprika, tomato puree, orange juice, parsley and wine. Cover and simmer until meat is tender. Add water if necessary. About 15 minutes before serving, add raisins, almonds, and olives. Serve with white rice.

Serves 4. *Mrs. Harold Tanenbaum (Dorothea)*

ROAST LEG OF LAMB WITH PEAR GARNISH

1 cup white wine
½ cup water
1 cup olive oil
1 tablespoon lemon juice
1 medium onion, chopped
2 cloves garlic, crushed
1 teaspoon tarragon vinegar
1 teaspoon crushed marjoram
1½ teaspoons salt

8 peppercorns, crushed
1 teaspoon rosemary, crushed
2 tablespoons flour

Garnish:
watercress
pineapple
kumquats
pears

Combine wine, water, oil, lemon juice, onion and garlic. Stir in vinegar, marjoram and remaining seasonings. Pour herb wine mixture over leg of lamb and let marinate over night. Place leg of lamb on rack in roasting pan and baste with marinade. Roast in slow oven 325° for 2½ hours or until meat thermometer registers 175° to 180°, depending on desired degree of doneness. Serve with herb gravy using pan drippings and flour and garnish with watercress, pineapple, kumquats and pears.

Serves 8 - 10. *Mrs. Sam Shapiro (Ruth)*

LAMB WITH CAPER SAUCE

leg of lamb
bay leaves
sliced lemon
onion

celery
rosemary
salt and pepper

Boil lamb in *well seasoned water* using the above ingredients. Cook
20 to 30 minutes to the pound.

Caper Sauce:
2 tablespoons butter
2 tablespoons flour
2 cups lamb stock
lemon slices

¼ teaspoon dry mustard
2 teaspoons vinegar
1½ tablespoons hot cream
4 tablespoons capers
2 or 3 hard boiled eggs

Make well seasoned cream sauce and adjust seasonings. When finished
add 4 tablespoons capers (I use almost a whole bottle plus putting
some of the juice in the cream sauce). Add chopped eggs. Cover lamb
with sauce and serve. Lamb can be cooked ahead and reheated.

Mrs. Sam Levy (Janis)
Mrs. H. F. Levy (Mary Lynne)
Montgomery, Alabama

WONDERFUL VEAL CHOPS

4 large veal chops
2 large Irish potatoes
1 large onion, sliced
salt and pepper

flour
cooking oil
1 cup hot water

Salt, pepper and flour chops. Brown quickly in hot oil. Remove meat
from pan and saute the onions in the skillet until limp. Add thinly
sliced potatoes and brown with the sliced onion. Add 1 cup of hot
water and then arrange chops on top of potatoes and onions. Cover
and steam for 20 minutes. Add salt and pepper to taste.

Serves 4.

Mrs. Leon Lewis (Esther)

VEAL MARSALA

2 pounds thin veal cutlets
4 tablespoons butter
flour
½ cup marsala (sweet sherry)

½ cup beef stock
salt and pepper
parsley

Flatten thin slices of veal, cut into 4 inch squares. Brown each side quickly in hot butter. Add broth a little at a time to keep meat moist while cooking. Add salt and pepper and sift a little flour over meat. When flour is browned, turn veal and repeat process. Add marsala and cover. Simmer about 5 minutes. Sprinkle with parsley and serve hot over rice. Mushrooms may also be added.

Serves 4.

Mrs. Jay Laskin (Eileen)

VEAL CORDON BLEU

6 thin pieces milk-fed veal
(approximately 4 x 6)
6 thin slices Swiss cheese
6 slices ham
3 eggs

seasoned bread crumbs
flour
salt and pepper, onion powder
to taste

Season veal with salt and pepper and onion powder. Put slices of cheese and ham over meat. Fold over carefully and secure tightly with skewer. Dip meat in seasoned crumbs and flour. Then dip in beaten eggs to which milk has been added. Dip back in seasoned crumbs. Fry slowly in two inches of shortening. When done, drain and serve hot.

This is especially good with candied sweet potatoes.

Serves 6.

Mrs. Bernard Perlmutter (Adele)

VEAL SCALLOPINE

¼ cup flour
½ cup parmesan cheese
1 teaspoon salt
⅛ teaspoon pepper
1½ pounds veal round
2 tablespoons olive oil

1 clove garlic
½ cup red wine
½ cup consomme
1 tablespoon lemon juice
chopped parsley

Wipe meat dry, mix first 4 ingredients and sprinkle over meat; then pound into meat well. Heat oil with garlic pod. Brown meat lightly on all sides. Add consomme, lemon juice and wine. Simmer covered till meat is tender. Sprinkle chopped parsley over top. Serve over broad noodles.

Serves 4 - 5.

Mrs. Gerald Katz (Doris)

VEAL CUTLETS PARMEGIANA

1½ pounds veal cutlets
  (cut ½ inch thick)
1 teaspoon salt
⅛ teaspoon pepper
2 eggs, slightly beaten

¼ cup grated parmesan cheese
½ cup sifted breadcrumbs
oil
1 cup tomato sauce
½ pound Mozzarella cheese

Divide cutlets into serving pieces ⅛ inch thick . Dip meat in eggs and then coat evenly with a mixture of parmesan cheese and crumbs. Brown cutlets on both sides in hot oil, allowing 3 minutes for each side. Place in shallow casserole or individual casseroles. Put a spoonful of tomato sauce on each, then a slice of cheese. Bake at 350° about 15 minutes.

Serves 4 - 6.

Mrs. Morton Seline (Anita)

PICKLED TONGUE

2 to 3 pound beef tongue
3 onions
2 bay leaves
2 cups vinegar
1 cup water

2 tablespoons brown sugar
2 tablespoons whole pickling
  spices
½ teaspoon salt

Boil tongue with 1 onion, bay leaves, and salt and pepper to taste. When tender, remove from heat and peal skin off tongue. Let stand until cold; slice tongue in thin slices. Place in layers in glass or china bowl alternating tongue and onions. Make brine of vinegar, water, brown sugar, pickling spices, and salt. Pour this mixture over layers of tongue and onions. Refrigerate for 36 hours. Serve as entree similar to pickled herring. May be served as an appetizer.

Mrs. A. S. Baer (Doris)

BARBECUE SAUCE I

1 stick butter, melted	garlic powder
¾ pint wine vinegar	onion powder
8 ounces pineapple juice	paprika
1 bottle chili sauce	cayenne pepper
4 tablespoons prepared mustard	black pepper
brown sugar to taste	½ cup water
lemon juice to taste	

Combine above ingredients. May be marinated in sauce several hours.

Mrs. Si Sartorius (Bunny)

BARBECUE SAUCE II

¼ cup vinegar	1 thick slice lemon
½ cup water	1 onion, peeled and sliced
2 tablespoons sugar	½ cup ketchup
1 tablespoon prepared mustard	2 tablespoons worcestershire
½ teaspoon pepper	sauce
1½ teaspoons salt	1½ teaspoons liquid smoke
¼ teaspoon cayenne pepper	(optional)

Mix first 10 ingredients in saucepan; simmer 20 minutes uncovered. Add ketchup and next 2 ingredients. Bring to boil.

Makes 1¾ cups.　　　　　*Mrs. Simon Frank (Hank)*

JULES BREITENBACH'S BARBECUE SAUCE

Cook together until done:
1 cup cooking oil
1 cup finely chopped onions

3 pods garlic, mashed through
   garlic press
1 lemon (rind and juice)

Then add:
½ cup prepared mustard
1 cup ketchup
1 cup worcestershire sauce
½ cup vinegar

salt and pepper to taste
1 cup water
1 teaspoon mixed pickling spice
½ bottle hot sauce

Let all boil together for about 15 minutes. Enough sauce to baste 12 fryers. This sauce will keep indefinitely, if refrigerated.

Mrs. Jules Breitenbach (Mickey)

HORSERADISH SAUCE

3 tablespoons margarine
3 tablespoons flour
1 cup milk
1 cup beef broth
2 tablespoons horseradish
   (may use more)

1½ teaspoons prepared mustard
½ cup snipped parsley
1½ teaspoons seasoned salt
2 egg yolks
6 tablespoons sour cream

Melt margarine and stir in flour, then add milk and broth. Bring to boil. Simmer one minute. Add horseradish, mustard, parsley, and salt. Remove from heat. Beat yolks, add sour cream. Stir into sauce. Put pan back on heat, and bring to boil. Serve over meat.

Mrs. Sam W. Levy (Grace)

POTTED BEEF ESTERHAZI

beef round (trimmed)
oil
1 or 2 cups white wine
garlic
capers and juice
salt and pepper

fresh vegetables (julienne
   carrots, celery, onions)
bay leaf
sour cream
blanched julienne lemon rind

Rub meat with salt, pepper, and oil. Place in 450° oven until brown. Reduce heat to 275°. Add wine. Cover pot. Turn meat occasionally. When meat is ¾ cooked add vegetables, garlic, and bay leaf. When tender remove meat and add to juices sour cream to taste, and a few capers with their vinegar. Boil. Correct seasonings. Add rind of lemon. Pour sauce over meat. Cover and keep warm.

Chef Foulard
Foulard's Restaurant

VEAL SCALOPPINE ANNEMINE

baby veal—thin slices
eggs—beaten well
lemon juice

butter
salt and pepper

Combine eggs and some of lemon juice. Dip veal in mixture. Saute swiftly in clarified butter. Season with salt and pepper. Place on serving platter. In same pan add more butter and a large quantity of lemon juice. Let boil rapidly (not fry) until sauce becomes the consistency of light cream. Pour over veal. Garnish with parsley. Serve immediately.

Chef Foulard
Foulard's Restaurant

MARINADE FOR BEEF KABOB

½ cup olive oil
2 tablespoons vinegar
2 tablespoons lemon juice
1 teaspoon dry mustard
¼ teaspoon thyme
½ teaspoon salt
¼ teaspoon pepper
¼ teaspoon oregano
1 tablespoon seasoning salt

3 cloves garlic, crushed
½ cup onion, chopped
2 tablespoons ketchup
1 teaspoon sugar
½ teaspoon marjoram
½ teaspoon rosemary
1 tablespoon worcestershire
  sauce
1 teaspoon chili powder

Bring to a boil and pour over 1 inch cubed sirloin tip. Refrigerate overnight, turning occasionally.

Serves 8.

Mrs. Art Casper (Cissy)

FOWL

BREAST OF CHICKEN GOLD

6 chicken breasts
beaten egg
bread crumbs

½ pint coffee cream
1 cup champagne
sauteed mushrooms

Skin, bone, and flatten (by hand) 6 chicken breasts. Dip in egg and bread crumbs, and saute in butter. Bake one hour at 350° in oblong pyrex casserole with ½ pint coffee cream and about a cup champagne. Add sauteed mushrooms. Serve with rice or noodles.

Serves 6.

Mrs. Irvin Shlenker (Bertha Alyce)

CHICKEN KIEV

(This is a very rich but very elegant entree.)

6 whole chicken breasts, boned
butter
1 cup milk
1 tablespoon flour
1 egg

½ teaspoon salt
1 cup sliced mushrooms
½ cup chopped chives
1½ cups sour cream

Bone chicken breasts and place a pat of butter between the two halves and tie with a string. Make a batter with milk and egg; roll breasts in seasoned flour, then in batter, and again in seasoned flour. Brown well in butter. Remove chicken. Add 1 cup sliced mushrooms to the butter, simmering for about a minute. Add 1½ cups sour cream and ½ cup chopped chives. Place chicken breasts in a casserole and pour sour cream mixture over. Bake at 350° until very hot. When ready to serve add shredded almonds and a little brandy.

Serves 6.

Mrs. A. A. Kaufman (Jean)

EASY BAR-B-Q CHICKEN

1 fryer
2 tablespoons worcestershire
   sauce
1 tablespoon vinegar

1 tablespoon kitchen bouquet
1 tablespoon sugar
½ cup ketchup
dash hot pepper sauce

Brown chicken well in butter. Remove to shallow baking dish. Combine remaining ingredients as a sauce and pour over chicken. Bake uncovered at 350° for one hour. Baste every ten minutes. Chicken will be very dark.

Serves 4.   *Mrs. Kenneth Margolis (Ann)*

CHICKEN COLUMBUS

2 fryers, disjointed
1 package slivered almonds

2 #2½ cans sliced peaches,
   drained
1 bottle French dressing

Salt and pepper chickens. Soak chicken in French dressing several hours. Put sliced peaches over chicken and bake in 375° oven two hours, turning chicken carefully. You may need to turn up the oven to 425° to brown the last twenty minutes.

Remove chicken and place on platter with peaches and gravy on top. Sprinkle almonds over top of peaches. Serve with rice cooked in onion soup.

Serves 6.   *Mrs. Bernard Perlmutter (Adele)*

CHICKEN IMPERIAL

1 large fryer chicken, cut up
1½ cups crushed salted crackers
1½ cups grated parmesan
   cheese
¼ cup chopped parsley

¼ cup grated onion
1 tablespoon salt
½ teaspoon pepper
½ cup melted butter
3 tablespoons butter

Combine crackers, cheese, parsley, onion, salt and pepper. Dip pieces of chicken in melted butter covering thoroughly; then coat thickly with cracker and cheese mixture. Place pieces skin side up in baking pan and dot with three tablespoons butter. Bake uncovered in preheated 375° oven for one hour or until tender.

Serves 4.   *Mrs. Arthur Simon, Jr. (Wilma)*

CHICKEN MAIN DISH

3 pounds chicken breasts
2 small cans water chestnuts,
   drained and sliced
¾ cup sauterne wine
2 cans cream of chicken soup

¼ cup water
½ cup chopped parsley
melted butter
paprika
salt and pepper

Brush chicken with melted butter, sprinkle with paprika and broil until brown. Arrange in a flat baking dish, season with salt and pepper. Blend liquids and pour over chicken, top with water chestnuts and parsley. Bake at 325° for 1½ hours.

Serves 4.   *Mrs. Morey Miller (Mae)*

CHICKEN POLYNESIAN STYLE

1 - 3 pound fryer, cut up
¾ cup honey
½ cup brown sugar
¼ cup orange or pineapple juice

¼ teaspoon ginger
⅛ teaspoon dry mustard
salt to taste

Place chicken in a shallow pan. Mix remaining ingredients together and brush on chicken. Sprinkle with paprika. Place under a broiler at 375°. Baste often until brown. Turn chicken and repeat until brown and chicken is glazed. Garnish with shredded coconut.

Serves 4.   *Mrs. S. W. Asher (Bettye)*

133

CHICKEN OREGANO

1 - 2½ to 3 pound fryer,
 disjointed
¼ cup oil
1 onion, chopped
1 large clove garlic, minced
1 teaspoon salt

¼ teaspoon pepper
1 tablespoon oregano
3 fresh tomatoes, diced
1 can (4 ounces) mushrooms,
 sliced or chopped

In a heavy skillet brown the chicken in oil over medium heat. Add onion and garlic; cook several minutes until vegetables are clear. Sprinkle with salt, pepper and oregano. Add tomatoes and mushrooms with juice. Cover and cook over low heat 30 minutes, until tender. If necessary, add a little water during cooking to insure spooning the delicious sauce over chicken when served.

Serves 4.   *Mrs. Jerry Bass (Phyllis)*

CHICKEN SAUTE

6 chicken breasts
salt and pepper
1½ tablespoons cornstarch
1 beef bouillon cube
1½ cups water

1 can mushrooms (fresh
 preferred)
dash lemon juice
1 tablespoon soy sauce
dash garlic powder
parsley

Season chicken breasts, saute in chicken fat or other mild fat until golden. Remove from pan. Cook mushrooms if using fresh ones and remove. Add the cornstarch to drippings, scraping up chicken bits. Add 1 beef bouillon cube and the 1½ cups water stirring until sauce is thick. Add soy sauce until sauce is rich dark brown. Add mushrooms, dash of lemon juice and dash garlic powder. Return chicken to pan, simmering for about 20 minutes. Spoon sauce over chicken frequently. To serve, put chicken breasts over mound of rice (could be wild rice). Spoon sauce with mushrooms over top. Garnish with parsley.

Serves 4 - 6.   *Mrs. Milton Gugenheim (Aileen)*

EAST INDIA CURRY

Day before:
4 - 4½ pound stewing chickens
6 cups hot water
2 onions

6 celery tops
2 tablespoons salt
2 bay leaves
2 carrots, pared

Cook chickens in hot water, seasonings and vegetables, until chickens are fork tender. Remove chicken from broth and save broth. When cool enough to handle, remove meat from bones and cut into fairly large pieces. Refrigerate. (You should have about 16 cups of meat.)

Day of serving:
⅔ cup butter or margarine
2 cups chopped onion
2 cups chopped celery
1⅓ cup flour

4 teaspoons curry powder
4 teaspoons salt
4 teaspoons pepper
10⅔ cups milk or 5⅓ cups milk
   and 5⅓ cups broth

In large kettle, melt butter; add chopped onions and celery; cook until lightly browned. Then stir in flour, curry powder, salt and pepper. Slowly stir in milk (or milk and broth). Cook until thickened, stirring constantly. Gently add chicken, and keep warm over low heat or over hot water.

Serves 20 - 24.   *Mrs. Ross Seline (Dee)*

CHICKEN AND RICE

1½ cups uncooked rice
6 fryer breasts
1 bottle Italian dressing

1 envelope onion soup mix
1 can cream of mushroom soup

Sprinkle rice in large baking dish. Dip breasts in dressing and place on rice. Pour remaining dressing over rice. Sprinkle onion soup mix over chicken and rice. Dilute mushroom soup with two cans water and pour evenly over other ingredients. Do not add any salt. Cover with foil. Bake for an hour and thirty minutes at 350°, removing foil for last fifteen minutes.

Serves 6.   *Mrs. W. Gold (Lillyan)*

CHICKEN IN WHITE WINE SAUCE
Coq au Vin Blanc

2 - 2½ pound fryers, quartered
4 tablespoons oil
½ cup onions, minced
1 carrot, grated
2 cloves garlic, minced
2 teaspoons salt
½ teaspoon pepper
1 bay leaf
3 tablespoons minced parsley
⅛ teaspoon marjoram
2 cups dry white wine
½ pound mushrooms, sliced
4 tablespoons butter
2 cloves (optional)
12 small white onions (canned may be used)
1 tablespoon or more cornstarch

Heat oil in casserole or Dutch oven and brown chicken. Add minced onion, garlic and carrots; saute for 10 minutes. Add salt, pepper, bay leaf, parsley, marjoram and wine. Cover and cook over low heat 10 minutes. Saute mushrooms in butter for 5 minutes. Stick cloves in one of the onions and add onions and mushrooms. Cover and cook over low heat about one hour or until chicken is tender. Mix cornstarch with a little cold water and blend into sauce. Cook, stirring steadily until thickened. Taste for seasoning.

Serves 6.   *Mrs. Albert Meyerson (Bertha)*

CHICKEN LIVERS WITH PINEAPPLE

4 slices pineapple
2 tablespoons oil
1 pound chicken livers
½ teaspoon salt
1 cup chicken broth
2 tablespoons cornstarch
2 teaspoons soy sauce
½ cup wine vinegar
½ cup sugar

Saute pineapple (cut into six pieces each) in oil. Remove from pan and add salted livers. When tender and slightly brown, remove to hot platter. Mix cornstarch to paste with a little chicken broth. Add soy sauce, vinegar, sugar and broth. Add to skillet. Cook and stir until mixture thickens and is clear. Add pineapple; heat thoroughly and pour over livers. Serve over rice.

Serves 3.   *Mrs. Jerry Rubenstein (Linda)*

MOTHER'S SIMPLE CHICKEN

This is a company dish made with chicken breasts. Made with whole cut up fryers it is a good family meal.

6 whole breasts of chicken, boned
6 green onions (shallots), cut very fine
6 tablespoons parsley, chopped very fine
1½ sticks butter
1 cup water
salt, pepper and paprika

Season chicken well with salt, pepper and paprika. Brown chicken in ½ stick of butter in 500° oven, turning once. Reduce oven heat to 350° and add remaining ingredients and cook for one hour. Serve over rice.

This recipe came from my mother. She cooked the chicken with the butter and parsley—I added the onion and water to make better and more gravy.

Serves 6.

Mrs. Frank Falkstein (Farnese)

SMOTHERED SQUAB

6 squabs
1 tablespoon salt
¼ cup butter or margarine
1 onion studded with cloves
black pepper
1 cup chicken consomme
1 tablespoon flour
1 tablespoon butter
½ teaspoon sugar
1 pinch nutmeg (optional)
1 small can tiny green peas

Rub squab inside and out with salt. Saute in butter until light brown all over. Remove to a casserole. Place remaining butter over squabs. Add onion and sprinkle with freshly ground pepper. Cover and bake at 325° for 40 minutes. Mix consomme with sugar, flour, remaining butter, nutmeg till thickened. Pour over squab, recover, bake 30 minutes longer. Add peas and bake additional 15 minutes. Place squab on heated platter, legs toward the center. Pour sauce over and sprinkle with chopped celery, 2 tablespoons hot brandy, light it (for company). Serve with tart jelly and wild rice.

Evelyn Landa Nixon

SQUABS WITH WILD RICE DRESSING

1 cup uncooked wild rice
2 tablespoons snipped parsley
¼ cup finely diced celery
¼ cup finely diced onion
1 small apple, pared and minced
1 teaspoon seasoned salt
6 - 1 pound ready to cook
   squabs

1 cup butter or margarine,
   melted
½ teaspoon salt
¼ teaspoon dried sage
¼ teaspoon dried thyme
2 - 10 ounce packages frozen
   broccoli spears (if desired)
Cumberland sauce
lemon slices

About 1 hour and 45 minutes before: In a saucepan place wild rice, snipped parsley, celery, onion, apple, seasoned salt, 2 cups water. Cook, covered, for 30 minutes. Drain if needed. Start heating oven at 500°. Use rice mixture to stuff squabs. With string tie legs together and bend back wings. Place squabs breast side up in a shallow open pan. In a saucepan combine butter, salt, sage, thyme; heat, then generously brush on the squabs. Bake uncovered for 15 minutes. Now lower heat to 400° and bake squabs 30 minutes longer or until tender with fork, basting every 10 minutes with drippings from pan. During last 15 minutes of baking, cook broccoli as package directs, then make Cumberland sauce (see recipe below). When broccoli is done, arrange down center of platter, tucking lemon slices here and there. Arrange squabs on either side, removing string. Pass sauce.

Sauce:
¾ cup currant jelly
½ cup orange juice

1 tablespoon instant minced
   onion
1 cup port wine

In a saucepan melt jelly. Add onion, orange juice and wine, stirring constantly. Heat to simmering point, then keep hot until serving time.

Makes 1½ cups sauce.

Serves 6.

Mrs. Bernard Sakowitz (Ann)

PICHONES CON ACEITUNAS
(Roast Squab with Ripe Olives)

6 squabs
clove of garlic
2 tablespoons of olive oil
2 onions, grated
6 carrots, grated
2 cups chicken stock

1 cup white wine
1 bay leaf
1 clove
1 cinnamon stick
12 pitted black olives

Heat 2 tablespoons olive oil with a clove of garlic; saute 6 squabs on all sides until they are golden. Remove the squabs to an earthenware casserole. In the same oil saute onions and carrots until vegetables just begin to change color. Add 2 cups chicken stock, 1 cup white wine, bay leaf, clove and cinnamon. Pour the sauce over the birds and season with salt and pepper. Bake in a slow oven at 300° for 1 hour, or until they are tender. Pour off the sauce; strain, and return to the casserole. Add 12 pitted black olives, reheat and serve the squabs immediately.

Serves 6.   *Mrs. George Bailes (Jean)*

QUAIL IN WINE

Rub quail with salt and freshly ground black pepper. Brown lightly in melted butter and place in buttered casserole. In skillet in which birds were browned, add 1 carrot diced, 1 small chopped onion, 2 tablespoons chopped green pepper, ½ cup chopped mushrooms, 3 small slices blanched orange peel.

Cook vegetables slowly for 5 minutes (stir), stir in 1 tablespoon flour, stirring constantly. Add 1 cup chicken stock until thickened, salt and pepper to taste. Simmer slowly for about 10 minutes. Pour ½ cup white wine (Rhine wine or sauterne) over quail. Place casserole in oven 350° for 10 minutes. Pour sauce over birds. Cover, cook 20 minutes or till tender.

Evelyn Landa Nixon

CANTONESE DUCK

4-6 pound duck
2 teaspoons salt
1 bunch green onions
¼ cup cornstarch
¼ cup water

¼ cup flour
salt and pepper
butter—to saute duck
bead molasses
soy sauce

Wash duck, removing skin and fat. Steam until tender using a pressure cooker. Sprinkle 2 teaspoons salt over the duck and cool. Bone it, handling it very gently. Sprinkle with flour. Saute each piece in butter until golden brown and crisp.

Gravy: combine ¼ cup cornstarch with ¼ cup water. Add two cups duck stock, diced duck giblets, 1 teaspoon soy sauce, 1 teaspoon or more bead molasses, ¼ cup green onions and tops, ¼ teaspoon black pepper. Cook until thick and simmer 7 or 8 minutes. Season more if necessary. Arrange on or around rice. Pour sauce over all. Sprinkle thickly with chopped green onions.

Serves 4 to 6.   *Mrs. Donald Butler (Jean)*

WILD DUCKS AND GEESE

1 cup vinegar
1 cup wine

1 teaspoon salt
water

Combine the above. Use enough water to cover game. Soak birds overnight, then throw away marinade.

Wash birds, dry, season with salt and pepper. Rub breast with butter and flour. If birds are not stuffed, use a small piece of apple, orange, celery, and onion in cavity of each bird. Put in greased baking pan. Start in a 350° oven—uncovered. Put chopped pieces of apple, orange, and celery in pan.

Sauce for Basting:
2 cups orange juice
1 can beef broth
salt and pepper to taste

2 tablespoons worcestershire
   sauce
¾ cup dry red wine

Baste every fifteen minutes with sauce. When birds are brown—takes about one hour—add rest of gravy. Cover and cook till done. Thicken gravy if necessary.

Mrs. Sam Levy (Grace)

WILD GAME SAUCE (DOVE, DUCK, GOOSE)

To prepare: When fresh killed, pick all feathers, remove all intestines, including lungs, which are under breast bone, wash thoroughly and put one small onion in cavity. Leave in refrigerator 24 hours. To cook: Remove onion from cavity and insert a fresh onion in cavity and leave inside throughout cooking period. Remove onion before serving.

Sauce:
6 ounces ketchup (1 cup)
6 ounces chili sauce
1 diced onion
4 tablespoons salt
1 teaspoon black pepper
1 teaspoon red pepper
2 bay leaves

1 lemon (juice)
1 stalk celery, cut fine
1 tablespoon pickling spice
1 tablespoon whole black
 pepper
1 cup sauterne or burgundy
1 tablespoon each bacon fat and
 shortening

Brown fowl in bacon fat and shortening in 475° oven, turning often, until very brown, add remaining ingredients (except wine) and 2 cups water. Cook until celery and onion are well done and birds are tender.

Add wine 10 minutes before serving.

Leon Kaufman
San Antonio, Texas

SAUCES FOR GAME

Warm 1 cup currant jelly with ½ cup port wine. Serve hot.

A jar of currant jelly, few dashes worcestershire, and a jigger of sherry. Serve hot over duck or as a sauce.

Evelyn Landa Nixon

SEAFOOD

FISH FILLET EN PAPILOTTE

4 (½ pound) fillets of sole
½ cup scallions
½ stick of butter
1 tablespoon flour
1 large tomato
¼ cup lemon juice
2 tablespoons sherry (dry white)

½ teaspoon oregano
½ teaspoon salt
½ teaspoon pepper
1 tablespoon Escoffier sauce
2 tablespoons cream or sour cream
1 can sliced mushrooms

Wash fish, dry, season lightly. Butter square of heavy duty foil. Place fillets on foil. Saute scallions lightly in butter, add flour and tomato, and rest of seasonings and stir. Cook slightly. Spoon over fish. Wrap tightly. Bake in 350° oven for 40 minutes.

Mrs. Sam W. Levy (Grace)

FISH PIQUANT

4 to 5 pound trout or red fish
garlic
celery

salt
red pepper
onion

Cover and boil whole fish in enough water to cover with the above ingredients. Cook until fish is tender. Remove from water and bone. Place a mound of fish on individual salad plates. Save broth.

Sauce:
butter the size of an egg
3 tablespoons flour
juice of 3 lemons
2½ cups fish broth

2 egg yolks, beaten
capers
chopped dill pickles
parsley

Melt butter and add flour, lemon juice and stir into the fish broth. Cook over low heat until thick. Remove and pour over well beaten egg yolks. Pour over fish and sprinkle generously with capers, pickles and parsley. Let cool but do not refrigerate as this forms a scum. Serve at room temperature.

Makes a delicious luncheon dish or fish course for a formal dinner.

Serves 10 - 12.

Mrs. A. A. Kaufman (Jean)

STUFFED FLOUNDER

1 fresh flounder
1 onion, chopped fine
2 ribs celery, chopped
¼ cup green pepper, chopped
butter
½ to 1 cup bread crumbs
1 pound fresh crab meat (lump preferred, but claw acceptable)
salt and pepper

Select a flounder, the size depending upon the number to be served. Have a pocket for stuffing cut in the top (dark) side of the flounder. Saute the vegetables in butter until clear. Add bread crumbs. Add 1 pound fresh crab meat and generous amount of butter to moisten. Salt and pepper to taste. Mix well. Fill the prepared pocket of the flounder, and pile the remaining dressing around the fish. Dot with butter and bake in a 375° oven for 1 hour. It is preferable to bake the fish in an ovenproof serving dish.

Serves 4-6 depending on size of fish.

Mrs. Milton Gugenheim (Aileen)

SHRIMP A LA CREOLE

1 clove garlic, minced
½ cup onion, chopped
1 tablespoon butter or margarine
1 tablespoon flour
6 large tomatoes, peeled and chopped
½ cup celery, chopped
1½ teaspoon salt
¼ teaspoon thyme
cayenne to taste
2 bay leaves
2 pounds raw shrimp, shelled

Saute onion and garlic in butter. Blend in flour. Add remaining ingredients except shrimp. Simmer 10 minutes. Add shrimp. Simmer 10 minutes again. Serve over rice.

Serves 6.   *Mrs. Al Crystal (Sara)*

SHRIMP ETOUFFEE

1 medium onion, chopped fine
2 green onions, chopped fine
3 or 4 cloves garlic, minced
¼ cup chopped celery
½ cup butter
2 tablespoons flour
2½ cups water
1 - 10½ ounce can tomato puree
2 bay leaves

1 tablespoon worcestershire
  sauce
4 drops tabasco sauce
1 teaspoon salt
½ teaspoon sugar
⅛ teaspoon pepper
1 to 1½ pounds shrimp, cleaned
  and raw

In a large skillet, saute onion, green onions, garlic and celery in butter until tender. Add flour. Cook and stir until lightly brown. Add water, tomato puree, bay leaves, sauces and seasonings. Simmer uncovered, stirring occasionally, 25 minutes. Add shrimp and continue cooking 15 minutes. Serve over rice.

Mrs. Leslie Moses (Eleanor)

SHRIMP deJONGHE

3 pounds shrimp, boiled and
  cleaned
1 teaspoon salt
2 cloves garlic, minced
¾ cup butter

1 cup bread crumbs
dash of cayenne and paprika
4 tablespoons parsley, minced
½ cup sherry

Mix garlic and salt. Cream with butter. Add remaining ingredients and place alternate layers of shrimp and bread crumb mixture in a buttered baking dish. Bake in hot oven 450° for 20 to 25 minutes. Serve as main dish or appetizer using toothpicks.

Mrs. Gerald Katz (Doris)
from *Mrs. Joseph Hirsch*
Baton Rouge, Louisiana

POLYNESIAN SHRIMP

3 eggs, beaten
½ cup flour
¼ cup cornstarch
¼ teaspoon salt
¼ teaspoon pepper

½ teaspoon garlic powder
1 teaspoon soy salt
1 pound large shrimp, cleaned
  and cooked

Mix together first 7 ingredients to make a thick batter. Dip shrimp quickly into batter and fry in deep fat until golden brown.

Sauce:
1 cup water
1 cup vinegar
1 cup sugar
2 large green peppers, cut in thin strips
1 large tomato, peeled and diced
1 cup pineapple, cubed (fresh or canned)

1 cup sweet pickles, diced
1 large carrot, sliced in thin rounds
½ cup mushrooms, pieces or small whole
¼ cup slivered almonds
Paste:
1 tablespoon cornstarch
2 tablespoons soy sauce

Cook first 3 ingredients until sugar dissolves and add remaining items and cook for two minutes. Mix cornstarch and soy sauce making a thick paste, and add to sauce mixture. As it thickens add fried shrimp and cook five minutes. Serve hot on bed of cooked rice.

Mrs. Sam Robinson (Ruth)

SHRIMP SCAMPI

1 pound large unshelled shrimp
Combine:
½ cup melted butter
1 clove garlic, minced

salt and pepper
2 tablespoons parsley, minced
2 tablespoons dry white wine

Slit shrimp down back, remove vein and place on baking pan. Pour sauce over shrimp and broil each side 5 minutes.

Mrs. Alan Gugenheim (Renee)

SHRIMP TEMPURA

1 cup sifted all-purpose flour
½ teaspoon salt
½ teaspoon baking powder
1 egg

¾ cup milk
2 tablespoons vegetable oil
2 pounds cleaned raw shrimp
   (butterflied)

To butterfly shrimp, start with raw shrimp and leave the tails intact when you clean them. Split along back curve cutting deep, almost to the inner edge. Open shrimp, then press flat to look like a butterfly. Sift flour, salt, and baking powder into small bowl. Add egg and milk. Beat until smooth. Beat in vegetable oil. Dip shrimp into batter, a few at a time, letting excess batter drain off. Fry in 1 inch of oil heated to 375°. Cook 2 to 3 minutes until golden brown. Drain on paper towels.

Serve with:

Sweet Sour Sauce:
1 tablespoon cornstarch
¼ cup sugar

¼ cup vinegar
¼ cup pineapple juice
2 teaspoons soy sauce

Mix cornstarch and sugar in small saucepan. Add vinegar, pineapple juice and soy sauce. Heat, stirring while sauce boils and thickens a bit. Use slices of fresh pineapple and parsley for garnish.

Serves 6.   *Mrs. Sol Rubenstein (Evelyn)*

SWEET AND PUNGENT SHRIMP

1 pound shrimp, cleaned and
   cooked
1 flat can pineapple, cut into
   pieces
½ cup brown sugar

½ cup vinegar
2 tablespoons soy sauce
3 tablespoons cornstarch
1 green pepper, cut into strips
1 fresh tomato, cut into wedges

Bring the pineapple syrup, soy sauce and ¾ cup water to a boil. Combine cornstarch with ½ cup water. Add to above and cook and stir until thickened. Add green pepper, tomato, pineapple and cook for 2 minutes. Put shrimp in sauce and heat thoroughly. Serve with rice.

Mrs. Joseph Engler (Rickey)

CURRIED SHRIMP

¼ cup butter
¼ cup flour
½ teaspoon salt
dash of paprika
1 teaspoon curry powder
dash of cayenne pepper

1½ cups milk
3 tablespoons ketchup
¼ cup sherry
1½ cups whole shrimp, cooked
2 cups rice, cooked

Blend butter, flour and seasonings, and gradually stir in milk. Cook until thick and smooth, stirring constantly. Add ketchup, sherry and shrimp. Serve over mounds of hot rice. Sprinkle with chopped parsley.

Serves 6.   *Mrs. Tobe Nathan (Etta)*

SEAFOOD SOUFFLE

9 slices bread, buttered
1 pound cheddar cheese, grated
Sauce:
1 can frozen shrimp soup
1 can milk
large jigger of sherry
½ teaspoon salt

4 eggs, beaten and added to
  sauce last
2 packages frozen crab meat (or
  2 cans king crab meat)
*Shrimp may be substituted or
  mixed

Grease casserole. Place layer of bread that has been trimmed and cubed on bottom, then cheese and crab meat. Cover layers with sauce. Place cheese on top.

Bake in 350° oven 1 hour. This must be prepared day or night before and refrigerated.

Serves 8 - 10.   *Mrs. Charles Freundlich (Bette)*
                                        from *Mrs. William Boas*
                                            Chicago, Illinois

BAKED CRAB

2 pounds fresh crab meat
2 onions, chopped
½ cup celery, chopped
¼ cup parsley, chopped
¼ pound butter

1 cup milk
1 to 1½ tablespoons flour
¼ teaspoon pepper
1 teaspoon worcestershire sauce
juice of 1 lemon

Saute onions and celery in butter. Add parsley and flour. Stir over medium heat until blended. Add milk and allow to cook 2 or 3 minutes until medium thick. Remove from heat. Add crab meat and seasonings. Place in casserole or individual shells. Top with packaged bread crumbs and dot with butter. Bake in 375° oven for 20 minutes.

Serves 8.   *Mrs. Bernard Perlmutter (Adele)*

STUFFED CRAB

1 pound lump crab meat
1 bunch green onions, chopped
4 ribs celery, chopped
¾ stick oleo or butter
¼ cup parsley, chopped

juice of one lemon
worcestershire sauce
ketchup
4 saltine crackers, crumbled
salt and pepper

Put butter in saucepan and saute onions and celery until light brown. In a bowl, put crab meat, crackers, salt, pepper, ketchup (just a couple of shakes), worcestershire sauce, and lemon juice and gently mix so that you do not break lumps. Add sauteed vegetables and parsley to crab meat mixture and gently mix. Place in shells. Add a few cracker crumbs on top with a small dab of butter. Bake at 350° for about 30 minutes or until very hot.

Mrs. Abe Zuber (Stella)

CRAB IN CREPES

Could be used as appetizer or dinner.

Crepes:
3 eggs, slightly beaten
1 cup milk

1 cup flour
½ teaspoon salt

Add milk, flour and salt to the eggs. Mix well. Drop by cooking-spoon full on lightly greased hot griddle. Brown on both sides. These should be paper thin.

Stuffing and Sauce:
½ medium onion, chopped fine
1 clove garlic, chopped fine
1 teaspoon dry mustard

worcestershire sauce to taste
3 tablespoons butter
1 pound lump crabmeat
salt and pepper to taste

Basic Cheese Sauce:
4 tablespoons butter
4 tablespoons flour
½ cup chicken broth

½ cup whipping cream
salt
3 tablespoons grated parmesan
    cheese

Basic Hollandaise Sauce:
½ cup butter
2 tablespoons water
4 egg yolks

¼ teaspoon salt
pinch of pepper
juice ½ lemon

Saute onions and garlic in butter. Do not brown. Add lump crab meat and saute. Add seasonings. Spread this filling in the crepe and roll like a tamale. Place in a baking dish.

Cover with cheese sauce (basic recipe) to which have been added two tablespoons of whipping cream and ⅓ cup of Hollandaise sauce (basic recipe). Put in oven and glaze.

Serves 6.   *Mrs. Jack Lapin (Susan)*

CRAB CASSEROLE

1 pound lump crab meat
1 stack (¼ of package) saltine
    crackers (crushed)
1 stick butter
2 cloves garlic, crushed

2 green onions with tops
½ pint half and half cream
salt and pepper
cayenne to taste

Saute onions in ¾ stick butter until transparent. Add garlic and cook slightly longer. Cool. Add ½ the crackers and the crab meat. Put in buttered casserole. Pour cream over top and sprinkle with remaining cracker crumbs. Dot with butter. Bake 25 minutes in medium oven.

Serves 4 - 6.   *Mrs. David Toomim (Shirley)*

CRAB IMPERIAL

½ pound shrimp, cleaned and
   cooked
1 can crab meat or ½ pound
   fresh
1 medium onion, chopped
1 cup celery, chopped

⅛ teaspoon pepper
½ teaspoon salt
1 teaspoon worcestershire sauce
1 cup bread crumbs (½ for
   mixture and ½ for top)
1 cup mayonnaise

Mix all ingredients together and place in shells or casserole. Bake 30 minutes in 350° oven.

Serves 4 - 6.   *Mrs. Simon Frank (Hank)*

LUMP CRAB MEAT VERMICELLI

1 pound lump crab meat
½ pound New York sharp
   cheese, grated

Sauce:
½ pound butter
¾ bottle ketchup
½ teaspoon dry mustard

½ pound vermicelli
1 medium size can sliced
   mushrooms
4 tablespoons worcestershire
salt and pepper
lemon juice to taste (sauce
   should be tart)

Place sauce ingredients in double boiler, cook and stir until well blended. Cook vermicelli, do not overcook. Butter casserole very well. Add layer of vermicelli, crab meat, cheese and mushrooms. Repeat ending with cheese on top. Pour sauce over all. Cover and place in pan of hot water. Bake in 350° oven for 40 to 45 minutes. Uncover the last 20 minutes. Sprinkle chopped parsley over top.

Serves 8.   *Mrs. Hans Katz (Irma)*

OYSTERS A LA ROCKEFELLER

6 sprigs parsley
6 spinach leaves
juice of one lemon
¼ cup sherry
4 green celery leaves

5 tops of green onions
½ teaspoon tabasco sauce
½ pound butter
1 dozen oysters

Grind all greens. Use pan to receive juices. (May use blender.) Melt butter, add lemon juice, sherry, tabasco and ground vegetables and juices. Fill tin pie pans with ice cream salt. Place in oven until hot. Remove and place large oysters in half shells that have been firmly pressed into salt. Pour a generous amount of vegetable mixture over each oyster. Place in oven. Let cook until oysters are heated through and edges curl, in 350° oven. Serve at once.

Mrs. Ivan Golden (*Bonnie*)

OYSTERS IN RAMEKINS

1 quart oysters
3 tablespoons butter
2 tablespoons flour
grated onion juice, small
    amount
1½ teaspoons Worcestershire
    sauce
¾ cup ketchup

1 cup oyster juice
¾ teaspoon salt
1 cup celery, diced
½ cup parsley, chopped
1 can tiny button mushrooms
few drops tabasco
cayenne pepper

Let oysters come to boil in own juice. Drain juice. Brown flour in butter, add onion juice and cook just a minute. Add worcestershire sauce and remaining ingredients. Taste for seasoning. Place in ramekins. Top with bread or cracker crumbs and butter. Brown slightly in oven.

Serves 10.

Mrs. Leopold Meyer (*Adeline*)

OYSTER SOUFFLE

3 tablespoons butter
3 tablespoons flour
pinch of salt
1 cup oyster liquid with milk
   added to make 1 cup

½ cup sharp cheese, grated
3 eggs, separated
1 dozen oysters
cracker crumbs, fine
paprika

Melt butter, stir in flour and salt and cook until thick, add cheese. Cool slightly and add beaten egg yolks. Roll oysters in cracker crumbs. Fold stiffly beaten egg whites into cheese mixture. In ungreased casserole, place alternate layers of oysters and sauce. Shake paprika on top. Bake in 325° oven until firm, about 30 minutes.

Serves 4.   *Mrs. Ted McWharf (Wanda)*

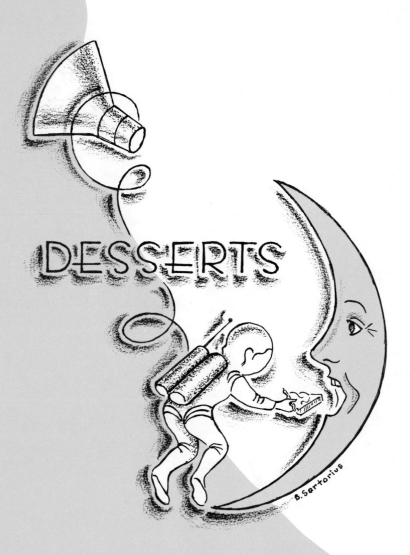

DESSERTS

APPLE COBBLER

5 cups sliced apples
½ cup white sugar

½ cup brown sugar
½ cup cream

Cover above mixture with crust.

Crust:
1¼ cups sifted flour
½ teaspoon salt

7 tablespoons shortening
3 tablespoons cold water

Bake in deep dish in a 400° oven 20-30 minutes.

Mrs. Henry Meyer (Ruth)

APPLE PIE FOR A LARGE CROWD

Double favorite pie crust recipe.

Line a jelly roll pan (10½ x 15½) with thin pie crust. Layer thinly sliced apples over the crust. Sprinkle with cinnamon-sugar mixture. Dot with butter. Make lattice top, but make the strips go straight across length and width. Bake 15 minutes at 450°, then 15-20 minutes at 350°, or until done. Cut in small squares to serve.

Serves 15.

Mrs. Milton Gugenheim (Aileen)

FUDGE PIE

⅓ cup butter
3 squares chocolate
4 eggs
2 cups sugar

¼ teaspoon salt
1 teaspoon vanilla
⅔ cup chopped pecans

Melt butter and chocolate in double boiler. Beat eggs, add sugar, salt, and vanilla blending well. Add to this chocolate and butter which has been slightly cooled. Add chopped pecans. Mix thoroughly. Pour into unbaked pastry shell and bake in 350° oven about 40 minutes.

Mrs. Joel Levy (Tudy)

FUDGE SUNDAE PIE

1 cup evaporated milk
1 package (small) semi-sweet
   chocolate bits
1 cup miniature marshmallows
¼ teaspoon salt

vanilla wafers
ice cream
pecans
whipping cream

Put milk, chocolate, marshmallows, and salt in a sauce pan over medium heat. Stir until mixture melts and thickens. Cool. Line bottom of 9 inch layer cake pan with vanilla wafers. Put a layer of ice cream, and ½ of chocolate mixture in pan. Repeat with wafers, ice cream, and chocolate mixture. Sprinkle pecans on top. Freeze. Garnish with whipped cream when ready to serve.

Serves 10.   *Mrs. Irvin Kaplan* (*Molly Ann*)

CHOCOLATE CHIFFON PIE

Crust: Use large box of vanilla wafers (roll or grind), 1 stick of melted butter. Mix thoroughly, and line the sides and bottom of a nine inch spring form pan.

Filling:
4 eggs
1 envelope unflavored gelatin
¼ cup cold water
½ cup boiling water

6 level teaspoons cocoa
¼ teaspoon salt
1 cup sugar
1 teaspoon vanilla

Dissolve gelatin in cold water. Mix cocoa and boiling water until smooth. Add gelatin to hot chocolate mixture and mix. To this mixture, add egg yolks slightly beaten with ½ cup sugar. Add vanilla Let cool. Add salt to egg whites and beat until stiff. Then add remaining ½ cup of sugar, and continue to beat until thoroughly mixed. When chocolate mixture starts to thicken, fold in egg white mixture. Place in refrigerator to set. Before serving, top with whipped cream (½ pint).

Serves 8.   *Mrs. Jules Breitenbach* (*Mickey*)

FRENCH SILK PIE

1 stick butter
¾ cup sugar
1 square bitter chocolate,
  melted
1 teaspoon vanilla

2 eggs
½ pint whipping cream
chopped pecans or shaved
  chocolate

Cream butter and sugar until light and fluffy. Add melted chocolate mixing well, add eggs — one at a time, beating five minutes after each addition. Add vanilla. Pour into baked 8 inch pie shell or crumb crust. Chill overnight. Top before serving with whipped cream sweetened with vanilla and sugar to taste. Sprinkle top with chopped pecans, or shaved bitter chocolate.

Serves 5 - 6.

Mrs. Gerald Katz (Doris)

GRASSHOPPER PIE

14 hydrox cookies, crushed
2 tablespoons butter, melted
½ teaspoon unflavored gelatin
2 tablespoons cold milk
24 marshmallows
½ cup milk

4 tablespoons creme de menthe
  (green)
2 tablespoons creme de cacao
  (white)
1 cup whipping cream, whipped

Combine crushed cookies and melted butter. Press on bottom and sides of buttered 8″ pan and chill. Reserve 2 teaspoons crumbs to spread on top of pie.

Sprinkle gelatin over cold milk and set aside. In double boiler melt marshmallows and ½ cup milk. Stir in creme de menthe and creme de cacao while marshmallows are still warm.

Add gelatin and milk mixture and cool. Set in refrigerator until slightly thickened, (about 10 to 15 minutes).

Add whipped cream to mixture, folding in gently. Pour into pie shell. Chill well before serving (about 4 to 5 hours). Can be made day before.

Mrs. Jake B. Sampson (Pauline)

HARLEQUIN PIE (Black Bottom)

3 cups chocolate wafers, crushed
6 tablespoons butter
2 envelopes gelatin
½ cup cold water
3 cups milk
6 eggs, separated
½ cup sugar

¼ teaspoon salt
4 tablespoons cornstarch
2 teaspoons vanilla
3 squares chocolate, melted
½ cup sugar
2 tablespoons rum
1 pint whipping cream

Mix crushed chocolate wafers and butter. Press into two 9 inch pie plates. Bake at 375° for 8 minutes. Cool. Add the cold water to the gelatin and set aside. Scald the milk in a double boiler. Slowly stir in the beaten egg yolks, ½ cup sugar, salt and cornstarch. Cook in double boiler over hot, not boiling, water until custard coats spoon. Remove. Add the gelatin. Stir until melted. To half of the custard add the vanilla and melted chocolate. Beat, cool until mixture stiffens and then chill. Chill remaining vanilla custard and fold in the 6 stiffly beaten egg whites to which you add ½ cup sugar and the rum. Place half of mixture into each crust. Spoon on chocolate mixture. Top with whipping cream.

Makes two 9 inch pies.

Mrs. M. M. Macow (Shirley)

LEMON PIE

3 eggs, separated
1 cup sugar
rind and juice of a lemon

1 teaspoon butter
½ cup warm milk
2 rounded teaspoons cornstarch

Combine egg yolks, sugar, rind and juice of a lemon in a double boiler. Cook over hot water. Slowly add warm milk in which cornstarch has been dissolved. Cook until thick. Pour into baked pie shell and top with meringue.

Meringue—3 egg whites stiffly beaten. Add to this 3 tablespoons sugar and beat until blended.

Mrs. Henry Meyer (Ruth)

LEMON CHIFFON PIE

4 eggs
1 cup sugar
juice of one lemon
1 lemon rind, grated

salt to taste
1 teaspoon unflavored gelatin
¼ cup cold water

Cook in a double boiler: the four egg yolks slightly beaten, ½ cup of sugar, lemon juice, rind and salt. Stir this frequently until the consistency of thick custard.

Soak the gelatin in the cold water and add to hot custard and cool. Beat egg whites stiff but not dry. Beat in the other ½ cup sugar gradually and then beat again. Fold cooled custard into beaten egg whites. Put in baked pie shell and chill 3 hours. Serve with whipped cream.

Mrs. Joel Levy (Tudy)
from
Stove's Restaurant
Marshaltown, Iowa

LIGHT 'N' AIRY STRAWBERRY PIE

1 - 10-ounce package frozen
   strawberries
1 envelope (1 tablespoon)
   unflavored gelatin
½ cup cold water
1 tablespoon lemon juice

dash of salt
2 egg whites
¼ cup sugar
½ cup heavy cream, whipped
red food coloring
graham cracker crust

Thaw strawberries. Soften gelatin in water. Heat over low heat, stirring constantly, till gelatin dissolves. Remove from heat. Add strawberries, lemon juice and salt. Refrigerate, stirring occasionally, till mixture stiffens slightly when spooned. Beat egg whites till soft peaks form, gradually add sugar, beating until stiff peaks form. Fold in gelatin, then whipped cream. Tint with red food coloring. Spoon into 9" graham cracker crust. Chill till firm.

Mrs. Herman Lapin (Maxine)

MERINGUE PIE

4 egg whites, beaten stiff   ¼ teaspoon cream of tartar
1 cup sugar

Mix in the order given and line the bottom and sides of a nine inch greased pie tin. Bake in a slow oven (275° F.) for one hour. Cool.

Filling: 3 tablespoons lemon juice
4 egg yolks   1 teaspoon lemon rind, grated
½ cup sugar   ½ pint whipping cream

Mix in the given order and cook in a double boiler eight to ten minutes. Cool. Whip the cream. Add half of cream to filling. Place in meringue crust and cover with remaining whipped cream. Chill in refrigerator for at least six hours before serving. If the meringue puffs out in baking, just press to pan.

Mrs. Harry Battelstein (Trudy)

MOCHA CREAM PIE

Bake your favorite pie crust to a light brown and cool.

Filling: 1 tablespoon cornstarch
½ cup sugar   1 cup milk
1 square bittersweet chocolate   ½ teaspoon salt
2 tablespoons instant coffee   1 teaspoon vanilla
3 tablespoons flour   1 cup whipping cream

Cook the sugar, chocolate, instant coffee, flour, cornstarch, milk and salt together, stirring constantly until thickened. Cool. Stir in vanilla. Whip cream until stiff and completely fold ⅔ into chocolate mixture. Then partially fold in the rest to get a marbled effect. Pour into baked pie shell.

Serves 8.   *Mrs. Milton Gugenheim (Aileen)*

ABBY'S PECAN PIE

1 cup white corn syrup
1 cup dark brown sugar
⅓ teaspoon salt
⅓ cup butter, melted

1 teaspoon vanilla
3 whole eggs
1 heaping cup shelled pecans

Mix syrup, sugar, salt, butter, vanilla. Mix in slightly beaten eggs. Pour into 9" unbaked pie shell. Sprinkle pecans over filling. Bake in 350° oven approximately 45 minutes.

Above is a specialty of the house at the Phoenix Hotel in Lexington, Kentucky.

Abigail Van Buren

SOUTHERN PECAN PIE

2 teaspoons margarine
1 cup dark brown sugar, firmly
  packed
2 teaspoons flour
1 cup light corn syrup

3 eggs, well beaten
1 cup pecan halves
1 teaspoon vanilla extract
¾ teaspoon salt
1 unbaked pastry shell

Heat oven to 400°. Work butter in a bowl until creamy. Stir in sugar and flour; mix well. Add syrup and eggs; beat until mixture is fluffy. Stir in nuts, vanilla, and salt. Pour mixture into shell. Bake 15 minutes and then lower heat to 350°. Continue to cook 30-35 minutes longer or until center is firm.

Serves 6 to 8.

Mrs. Barry Russak (Judy)

WHIPPED CREAM CHEESE PIE

1 - 8-ounce package of cream
  cheese
½ cup powdered sugar
½ pint whipping cream
⅓ cup granulated sugar

1 teaspoon vanilla
graham cracker crust
1 can blueberry or cherry
  prepared pie filling

Beat cream cheese well with powdered sugar until fluffy. Whip cream with granulated sugar. Fold whipped cream mixture into cheese mixture, add vanilla and pour into graham cracker crust. Chill. Spread prepared pie filling carefully over chilled pie and chill again for several hours before serving.

Mrs. Seymour Nathan (Gertie)

PUMPKIN ICE CREAM PIE

graham cracker crust (baked 9″
  pastry shell)
¼ cup honey or brown sugar
¾ cup canned or cooked mashed
  pumpkin
½ teaspoon cinnamon

¼ teaspoon ginger
dash each of nutmeg and cloves
¼ teaspoon salt
1 quart vanilla ice cream
⅓ cup broken pecans—optional

Combine honey, pumpkin, spices and salt. Bring to a boil, stirring constantly. Cool. Beat into softened vanilla ice cream; add nuts if desired. Spread into baked shell. Freeze until firm. Top with whipped cream and pecan halves if you like.

Mrs. H. Paul Levy (Norma)

PIE CRUST

(This recipe cannot be cut down.)

3 cups flour
1 cup shortening

¾ cup cold milk
1 teaspoon salt, mix with flour

Crumble flour, salt, and shortening to the consistency of corn meal. Pour in cold milk and quickly blend and stir until it holds together. Put in refrigerator covered for 2 hours or more. Roll to desired thickness.

Makes one double crust and one shell, or three shells.

Mrs. Milton Scheps (Joni)

ALMOND SPONGE

1½ envelopes plain gelatin
6 eggs, separated
1 cup sugar, heaping
1¼ cup hot milk
almond flavoring, approximately 1 teaspoon

pinch salt
1½ dozen crumbled macaroons
graham cracker shell or follow recipe on graham cracker box and make the crust first

Dissolve gelatin in a little cold water, then place pyrex cup in a skillet with water and dissolve until it is liquid. Beat egg yolks until light and fluffy. Cream in sugar but not all, then add hot milk. Cook in double boiler until thick. Let cool and then add almond flavoring and gelatin and crumbled macaroons. Fold in beaten egg whites with remaining sugar. Pour custard into graham cracker shell and refrigerate overnight.

Mrs. Sam Suravitz (Juanita)

BAKED BANANA HAWAIIAN

4 peeled bananas
½ cup firmly packed brown sugar
¼ cup pineapple or orange juice

3 tablespoons sherry
½ cup chopped Macadamia nuts
2 tablespoons butter

Place bananas in small baking dish. Pour mixture of sugar, juice, and wine over them. Sprinkle with nuts (sauteed in butter) and add pinch of nutmeg. Bake 350° about 15 minutes or until glazed.

Mrs. Leon Weiner (Sandra)

BAKED BANANAS

3 tablespoons butter
6 tablespoons sugar
3 tablespoons lemon juice

6 bananas
3 tablespoons rum or sherry

Melt butter. Add sugar and lemon juice, stir until well blended and remove from heat. Place peeled bananas in shallow baking dish. Sprinkle with rum or sherry. Then pour on butter sauce and bake at 350° for 30 minutes. Baste several times with butter sauce. Optional — Serve over ice cream when slightly cooled.

Mrs. Gene Burke (Jean)

MOTHER'S ALMOND TORTE

Line spring form with a Graham cracker crust. Bake crumb crust at 350° for 10 minutes.

Soak 2 envelopes plain gelatin in a little cold water. Dissolve over hot water.

Cook a custard of:
8 egg yolks

1 cup sugar
1¾ cups scalded milk

Beat egg whites stiff; add ½ cup sugar, then the custard, then the gelatin and 2 dozen crumbled almond macaroons. Use almond flavoring to taste.

Place in mold and refrigerate. When ready to serve, top with whipped cream and shaved and toasted almonds.

Mrs. Henry Desenberg (Helen)

BISQUE TORTONI

3 half pints whipping cream
3 dozen almond macaroons
12 egg yolks

12 tablespoons sugar
2 teaspoons vanilla

Cream egg yolks only with sugar until stiff. Beat cream until stiff. Add crumbled macaroons and vanilla. Mix all and pour into a pan from which water has been shaken. Freeze overnight or longer and serve topped with fruit either fresh or frozen.

Mrs. William Ladin (Lois)

BREAD PUDDING

3 poppy seed rolls
3 cups warm milk
3 eggs
1 cup sugar

pinch salt
grated rind of lemon
1 teaspoon vanilla

Soak the poppy seed rolls in the warm milk. Mash thru strainer. Beat yolks of eggs, add one cup of sugar, pinch of salt, grated rind of lemon and a teaspoon of vanilla. Mix well. Add the bread and milk mixture. Beat the egg whites stiff and fold into mixture. Bake in well greased pyrex dish in 325° oven for 30 minutes.

Serves 5 - 6 people.

Mrs. Raymond Cohen (Alyda)
Mrs. Mell Jacobs

FLAMING CHERRIES

1 cup drained pitted red
   cherries

¾ cup currant jelly
½ cup brandy

Melt currant jelly in top of chafing dish on stove. Stir well. Add pitted cherries, heat until it simmers, stirring slightly. Pour brandy into center of mixture. Do not stir. Heat and ignite. Place skillet on chafing dish and bring to table. Serve over ice cream.

Serves 6.

sent by *Mrs. B. Sanford*
Mrs. L. M. Landa, Jr. (Lois)

BAKED CUSTARD

A smooth custard, worthy of the most distinguished guests and highly reminiscent of those served in French restaurants.

5 whole eggs
4 egg yolks
3¾ cups of scalded milk

¾ cup sugar
1 tablespoon vanilla

Beat eggs well with sugar. Add hot milk slowly, mixing well. Add vanilla.

Burnt Sugar or Caramelized Topping

½ cup sugar   2 tablespoons water

Shake these in saucepan over medium heat till water is gone and sugar is golden brown. Quickly spread this over sides and bottom of souffle pan or pyrex baking dish. Pour custard over this. Bake in pan of water at 350° for 40 minutes. Let custard cool in dish, then invert on large round platter.

Mrs. Frank Lipper (*Nanette*)

CABINET PUDDING

9 eggs
1¼ cups sugar
water glass full of sherry wine
1 tablespoon gelatin
½ cup cherries, chopped

12 almond macaroons,
  crumbled
chopped pecans (as many as
  desired)
2 slices of crystallized pineapple, shredded

Separate eggs. Cream yolks well with sugar and add sherry. Put in top of double boiler and stir occasionally until thick. Meanwhile dissolve gelatin in cold water. When custard is partially cooled add gelatin. Allow custard to completely cool and fold in stiffly beaten egg whites. Use either sherbet glasses or bowl to mold in, putting a little of the custard in first and alternating with the macaroon pieces, nuts, and fruit. Top with whipped cream.

May be made in mold and turned out and sliced. I usually make it in a cut glass bowl and serve on a dessert plate and then add whipped cream.

Mrs. Ike L. Freed (Sybil)

CHOCOLATE ICE CREAM CUPS

6 ounce package of semi-sweet
   chocolate pieces
ice cream

whipping cream
maraschino cherries

Melt a 6 ounce package of semi-sweet chocolate pieces in a double boiler. When completely melted, allow to cool just slightly. Pour one tablespoon of melted chocolate into a fluted (paper) baking cup and spoon mixture to the sides of cup. Chill for an hour before peeling paper off. Fill chocolate cups with ice cream, top with spoon of whipped cream and a maraschino cherry. Refreeze until served.

Makes 6. *Mrs. John Landa (Nancy)*

CHOCOLATE MARSHMALLOW PUDDING

½ cup water
1 package gelatin
1 cup milk
¼ pound bitter chocolate
12 marshmallows

5 eggs, separated
1 cup sugar
whipped cream
shredded fresh coconut

Soak gelatin in water for 10 minutes, then put over boiling water to dissolve. Dissolve chocolate in milk over boiling water and cook until thickened. Add marshmallows and stir until dissolved. (Chocolate mixture *must* be allowed to cool before mixing last ingredients.) Cream yolks of eggs with sugar. Add chocolate mixture, then gelatin, and lastly add beaten egg whites. Pour into a greased mold and let set in refrigerator over night. Ice with whipped cream and shredded fresh coconut.

Mrs. Henry Desenberg (Helen)

CHOCOLATE ICEBOX CAKE

3 packages ladyfingers, plain
2 packages German sweet
  chocolate
4 eggs
1 pint milk

½ pint whipping cream
¾ cup sugar, scant
1 tablespoon flour mixed with
  sugar
1 teaspoon vanilla

Separate ladyfingers, cutting enough off so that ladyfingers will line the sides of flat bottom spring form pan. Also line bottom. Melt chocolate in top of double boiler. Beat eggs well, add sugar mixture and blend well. Heat milk (scald). When chocolate is melted, remove from stove and stir in egg, sugar mixture and then hot milk. Mix and put back over boiling water and cook, stirring slowly, keeping mixture from adhering to side of pan. Let thicken, then remove from stove and mix in vanilla. Spoon one half of chocolate custard carefully over ladyfingers in bottom of pan. Put additional ladyfingers over this, then rest of custard and finish with ladyfingers. Let cool, cover with foil and refrigerate at least 8 hours. When ready to serve, remove cake to serving plate and top with whipped cream.

Mrs. Henry Wexner (Helen)

CHOCOLATE TORTE

2 cups pecans, grated
4 egg yolks
1 cup sugar
2 tablespoons flour
½ teaspoon salt
½ teaspoon baking powder
1 tablespoon rum

4 egg whites
½ pint sweetened, flavored
  whipped cream
Topping:
6 ounce package semi-sweet
  chocolate
½ cup sour cream

Add sugar to egg yolks, cream well. Stir in flour, salt, baking powder, and rum. Add grated pecans to mixture. Beat egg whites till very stiff and fold in. Bake in 2 greased, lined 8-inch pans at 350° for 25 minutes.

For Topping: Melt chocolate in double boiler; add pinch of salt; mix with sour cream.

Put layers together with the whipped cream and topping mixture; top with grated pecans.

Mrs. David Toomim (Shirley)

CHOCOLATE ROLL

3 tablespoons cocoa
½ cup sugar

5 eggs, separated

Beat yolks, add sugar and cocoa. Beat whites stiff and fold in yolks. Bake 10 minutes in 350° oven in floured cookie tins. Turn out on floured towel. When cool fill with whipped cream or ice cream and roll.

Mrs. Albert Meyerson (Bertha)

CHOCOLATE SAUCE

4 squares unsweetened
    chocolate
½ stick butter
1 cup sugar

1 teaspoon baking powder
½ cup milk
1 teaspoon vanilla

Melt all ingredients in saucepan over low heat.

Mrs. Irion Heyman (Frances)

CHOCOLATE SAUCE

2 cakes German sweet chocolate
1 square bitter chocolate

½ pint coffee cream
½ cup sugar

Put all ingredients together using ½ of the cream. Melt and keep adding in small amounts the balance of cream until desired thickness is reached. Serve warm.

Serves 6.

Mrs. Charles Strauss (Florence)

HOT CHOCOLATE SAUCE

4 squares unsweetened
   chocolate
5 tablespoons sugar

30 marshmallows
¼ pint cream

Melt chocolate and cream in double boiler. Add sugar and marshmallows. Stir and melt all. Stir occasionally, and may add more sugar or cream, depending on how sweet or how thick you want it.

Wonderful to serve over cake with ice cream, or over filled kisses.

Serves 6 to 8.   *Mrs. Raymond Cohen (Alyda)*

BITTERSWEET-CHOCOLATE SAUCE

8 squares unsweetened
   chocolate
2 cups sugar
14½ ounce can evaporated milk

2 tablespoons strong black
   coffee
dash salt
1 teaspoon vanilla

Melt chocolate in top of double boiler over boiling water; add sugar; mix well. Cover and cook over boiling water for ½ hour. Add milk, coffee, salt and vanilla; beat until smooth and thick. Serve hot.

If desired, make ahead, cool and refrigerate. Will keep several weeks. Reheat over boiling water.

Makes 3 cups.   *Mrs. Samuel Simkin (Helen)*

FRENCH CHOCOLATE SOUFFLE

1½ squares unsweetened
   chocolate
⅓ cup sugar
2 tablespoons hot water
1 tablespoon butter

1 tablespoon flour
¾ cup milk
3 eggs, separated
1 tablespoon vanilla
¼ teaspoon salt

Melt chocolate over hot water; add sugar and water; stir until smooth. Melt butter; add flour and blend. Stir milk slowly and cook until boiling. Add chocolate and salt. Add to yolks; heat until thick.

Beat whites stiff and gently fold into mixture; add vanilla. Set in pan of hot water and cook 30 to 40 minutes in a 325° oven.

Serve at once. Use souffle dish and serve whipped cream with it.

Serves 6 - 8.   *Mrs. E. H. Gerson (Deeda)*

FUDGE CUPS

½ cup butter
1 cup sugar
1 egg, unbeaten
2 squares (2 ounces) unsweetened chocolate, melted

¼ teaspoon salt
¼ teaspoon red food coloring
2 cups sifted flour
whole pecans

Cream butter. Gradually add sugar, creaming well. Blend in egg; beat well. Add unsweetened chocolate, melted and cooled. Add salt and food coloring; blend well. Blend in flour; mix well. Chill about 1 hour. Shape into balls using a rounded tablespoon for each. Place in greased or paper lined muffin tin. Flatten and press dough about ½ inch up sides of cups. Bake at 350° for 8 to 10 minutes. Remove from pan and cool completely. Fill with fudge and top each with pecan.

Fudge Filling:
1½ cups sugar
⅓ cup milk
¼ cup butter
3 tablespoons light corn syrup

1½ squares unsweetened chocolate
⅛ teaspoon salt
1 teaspoon vanilla

Cook all ingredients over low heat until chocolate and butter melt. Bring to boil and boil 1 minute. Remove from heat and add vanilla. Beat until lukewarm and fill cups.

Mrs. Ivan Golden (Bonnie)

CHOCOLATE SOUFFLE

½ cup milk
2 tablespoons flour
1 tablespoon butter
2 tablespoons water

2 eggs (beat yolks & whites
  separately)
1 square bitter chocolate
3 tablespoons sugar

Heat butter, add flour, then milk. Cook until smooth. Add water and sugar to chocolate; heat and when chocolate is shiny, mix with milk sauce. Let cool then stir in beaten yolks and fold in stiffly beaten whites.

Pour into greased casserole. Set in pan of hot water and bake in 325° oven for 30-40 minutes. Test with knife—if comes clean it is done.

Serve hot and with Brandy Sauce.

Hot Brandy Sauce:
½ cup butter
1 cup sugar

1 whole egg
3 to 4 ounces cognac or may use
  bourbon whiskey

Cream butter and sugar. Stir over hot water until melted. Add beaten egg and a little water. Stir until thick. Add cognac.

Serve hot. Pass to pour over souffle after it is served.

Mrs. A. A. Kaufman (Jean)

QUICK DOBOSCH TORTE

1 (6 ounce) package semi-sweet
  chocolate pieces
2 tablespoons confectioners
  sugar
¼ cup boiling coffee
4 egg yolks

¼ pound margarine, thinly
  sliced
2 tablespoons dark rum
1 (2 pound) prepared pound
  cake

Put chocolate into electric blender and blend at high speed for six seconds. Turn off motor, scrape sides of glass. Add coffee and blend 6 seconds more. Add sugar, egg yolks, margarine and rum and blend 30 seconds.

Slice pound cake into 6 or 7 layers with a bread knife. Put layers back together with the chocolate mixture between each. Frost top and sides smoothly with chocolate mixture.

Store in refrigerator. Keeps moist for more than a week.

Mrs. Gus Block (Gay)

FORGOTTEN DESSERT

5 egg whites
¼ teaspoon salt
½ teaspoon cream of tartar

1½ cups sugar
1 teaspoon vanilla

Beat 5 egg whites until foamy. Add ¼ teaspoon salt and cream of tartar. Beat now until the egg whites stand in soft peaks, add 1½ cups sugar very gradually and keep on beating until the egg whites are stiff. Flavor with 1 teaspoon vanilla.

Grease and flour a 9 inch pie pan. Spread the meringue on the bottom, having it high around the edge and scooping it out in the center to form a shell. Have oven pre-heated to 400°. Place meringue in the oven and turn off the heat immediately. Leave in oven overnight. Do not open the oven. If prepared in the morning allow at least 4 or 5 hours with heat off.

Filling:
⅓ cup flour
¾ cup sugar
pinch salt

2 cups light cream
2 whole eggs
1½ teaspoons vanilla

Mix flour with three-fourths cup sugar and a little salt. Add well beaten eggs to cream. Beat this mixture into the dry ingredients gradually and continue beating well. Cook in top of double boiler over hot water, stirring constantly until thick and smooth. Cool and add 1½ teaspoons vanilla. Serve cold. Cover if desired with berries.

Mrs. Louis M. Landa, Sr. (Adeline)

177

CREAM PUFFS

¼ cup liquid shortening   ¼ teaspoon salt
½ cup boiling water   2 eggs
½ cup sifted flour

Combine shortening and water in saucepan. Heat until shortening melts to bubbling point. Add flour and salt all at once, stirring vigorously, cook until mixture leaves side of pan. Remove and cool 1 minute. Add eggs one at a time beating with spoon until smooth. Drop by wet teaspoon 2 inches apart on a greased cookie sheet, shaping with spoon into rounds that point up in center. Heat oven to 450°. Bake 10 minutes. Lower to 400° for 25 minutes. Do not open oven. Should be puffed high and golden brown. Cool, then cut off tops. Fill with ice cream, top with chocolate sauce or whipped cream.

Makes 8 medium or 4 large puffs.   *Mrs. Ted McWharf (Wanda)*

ICE CREAM PISA CAKE

3 packages plain ladyfingers   ½ gallon pistachio ice cream
½ gallon coffee ice cream   1 jar or can of chocolate syrup
½ gallon chocolate ice cream

Line a 12 inch spring form with ladyfingers. (Cut the ends of the ladyfingers flat so they will stand against the pan.) Let coffee ice cream become fairly soft, then smooth into spring form until it is half full. Set in freezer for several hours until frozen solid. Add jar or can of chocolate syrup over layer of ice cream. Put back into freezer and let freeze solid again. Allow chocolate ice cream to become soft, then add it to the cake and let it freeze solid. Allow the pistachio ice cream to soften, add it to the cake and freeze again. May be served with hot fudge sauce if desired, but before serving, allow to stay at room temperature a few minutes to become soft enough to cut with a sharp knife.

Makes approximately 20-24 medium slices.

Mrs. Ben Battelstein (Virginia)

COFFEE ICEBOX CAKE

50 marshmallows
1 cup *strong* coffee

1 pint whipping cream
3 dozen ladyfingers, split

Butter 9 inch spring form. Line bottom and sides with split ladyfingers. Melt marshmallows and coffee over water. Allow coffee mixture to chill until it is thick. Fold in whipped cream. Pour mixture over ladyfingers, alternate layers, ending with coffee mixture. Chill. Best if made 24 hours in advance.

Mrs. Richard Marks (Nonie)

MOCHA ICEBOX PIE

1 cup fine graham cracker
  crumbs
¼ cup melted butter or
  margarine
1 envelope unflavored gelatin

½ cup cold water
½ cup sugar
2 tablespoons instant coffee
¼ teaspoon salt
1 cup evaporated milk

Press on bottom of an 8 inch square pan a mixture of one cup fine graham cracker crumbs and ¼ cup melted butter or margarine. Chill until needed.

In a one-quart saucepan soften one envelope unflavored gelatin in ½ cup cold water. Add ½ cup sugar, two tablespoons instant coffee and ¼ teaspoon salt. Stir over medium heat until gelatin and sugar dissolve. Take off heat.

Stir in one cup evaporated milk. Chill in small bowl or electric mixer (or 1½ quart bowl) until firm. Beat with electric mixer at low speed until mixture is broken up. Beat in ⅔ cup evaporated milk.

Beat at high speed until mixture fills bowl. Pour over crumbs in pan. Sprinkle chocolate decorettes or shaved chocolate over top. Chill until firm about one hour.

Mrs. Jerry Sherman (Ruth)

ICEBOX CAKE

¼ pound unsalted butter
1 cup sugar
3 eggs, separated
juice of 1 orange

juice of ½ lemon
½ pint whipping cream
2½ dozen ladyfingers
2 dozen macaroons

Cream butter and sugar well. Add unbeaten egg yolks and fruit juices, stir lightly. Whip egg whites until stiff and add to above mixture. Whip cream and add.

Line spring form pan with ladyfingers and then alternate custard, macaroons and ladyfingers. Top with additional whipped cream.

Serves about 10.   *Mrs. Henry Meyer* (*Ruth*)

LEMON CHIFFON ICEBOX CAKE

8 eggs, separated
¾ cup sugar
rind of 2 lemons
juice of 3 lemons
½ cup cold water

1 envelope plain gelatin plus
   one teaspoon
10 marshmallows
½ cup sugar
2 packages ladyfingers

Beat egg yolks lightly in mixer with ¾ cup sugar and boil, adding rind of lemons and lemon juice. Dissolve gelatin in cold water. This is cooked and mixed in top of double boiler. Remove from heat and add marshmallows, dissolve and then cool. Beat egg whites with ½ cup sugar and fold into cooled mixture. Pour into ladyfinger lined spring form pan.

Mrs. Albert Meyerson (*Bertha*)

HEATH BAR DESSERT

3 pints whipping cream
3 dozen ladyfingers
1 heaping tablespoon instant coffee

12 Heath bars
2 tablespoons powdered sugar
8 x 13 pyrex pan

Butter pan and line bottom and sides with split ladyfingers. Whip cream and add coffee and powdered sugar. Then crack Heath bars in their package with a hammer into small bits. Add to whipping cream mixture. Put over ladyfingers, making two layers. End with whipping cream and decorate with shaved bitter chocolate. Make day before and refrigerate.

Serves 10 to 12.   *Mrs. David Brofman (Joanna)*

PECAN DELIGHT

22 Ritz crackers
3 egg whites
1 cup sugar

2 teaspoons baking powder
¾ cup pecans, chopped

Preheat oven to 350°. Crush crackers until fine. Beat egg whites until frothy. Gradually add sugar until peaks form. Blend in crumbs, baking powder, and nuts. Place in buttered 9 inch pie plate. Bake 25 minutes. Chill and serve with sweetened whipped cream or ice cream.

Serves 8.   *Mrs. Thomas Freundlich, Jr. (Cecile)*

QUICK EASY DESSERT

1 banana for each person
cinnamon and sugar (mixed)

butter
canned or fresh grated coconut

Peel banana, slice down center. Butter each side, sprinkle with cinnamon and sugar. Top with coconut. Broil under broiler for 5 minutes or until coconut has slightly browned. Serve immediately.

Mrs. Lew Harris (Henny)

PINEAPPLE CUPCAKES

(Quick and Easy)

1 stick butter
1 cup sugar
1 small can crushed pineapple

2 cups flour
2 teaspoons baking powder
2 eggs

Mix all ingredients together. Pour into paper lined muffin pans and bake in 350° oven. Sprinkle with sugar while warm.

Mrs. H. Levy (Elsie)

ICED STRAWBERRY SOUFFLE

3 pints hulled fresh strawberries
  (or two 1 pound packages
  frozen whole strawberries
  in heavy syrup)
1 cup granulated sugar
3 envelopes unflavored gelatin

2 tablespoons lemon juice
8 egg whites
¼ teaspoon salt
½ cup granulated sugar
2 cups heavy cream

Tie a 30" x 6" band of waxed paper around outside of a 7½" x 2⅔" (1½ quart) porcelain souffle dish so it stands 3 inches above rim.

Make 3½ cups strawberry puree by putting strawberries through blender at high speed. In saucepan, combine 1 cup sugar, gelatin, and add 1¾ cups of the strawberry puree. Stir over medium heat till gelatin is completely dissolved. Let cool. Add lemon juice and remaining puree. Chill over ice water stirring constantly, until it is like unbeaten egg whites, then remove.

In large electric mixer bowl at high speed, beat egg whites with salt until light and foamy, then gradually add ½ cup sugar, while beating until egg whites hold soft peaks. Pour egg white mixture into a 4 quart mixing bowl. Whip cream until cream holds its shape; pour over egg whites. Now add chilled puree.

With a rubber spatula, carefully blend all ingredients; then pour into souffle dish. Refrigerate 3 hours or until set. Then carefully remove waxed paper band. Serve with frozen strawberries, thawed and sliced, or unsweetened whipped cream.

Makes 10 - 12 servings.

Mrs. Stanford Alexander (Joan)

STRAWBERRY ROLL

½ cup cold water
2 eggs, separated
1 cup sifted sugar
sliced fresh or drained frozen
  strawberries

1 cup sifted cake flour
¾ teaspoon baking powder
¼ teaspoon salt
1 teaspoon vanilla

Add water to egg yolks, beat until foamy and triple in volume. Add sugar gradually, still beating until thick and lemon colored. Sift flour, baking powder, and salt; stir gently into yolk mixture with vanilla. Beat whites stiff, fold into yolk mixture. Bake in jelly roll pan lined with wax paper and greased at 350° for about 20 minutes. Turn out on cloth covered with powdered sugar, roll, let cool. Unroll, spread with sweetened whipped cream and strawberries. Roll again and chill. Could also be filled with other fruits or various pie fillings.

Mrs. Robert E. Caine (Sunny L.)

SWEDISH CREAM

2⅓ cups heavy cream
1 cup sugar
1 envelope of gelatin

1 pint sour cream
1 teaspoon vanilla

Mix together heavy cream, sugar, and gelatin. Heat gently, and stir until gelatin is completely dissolved. Cool until slightly thickened. Fold in sour cream and flavor with vanilla. Chill in refrigerator until firm. Spoon into serving dishes and top with sweetened fresh fruit or berries.

Serves 6.

Mrs. Sam W. Levy (Grace)

TUTTI FRUITTI SHERBET

3 cups orange juice
1 cup lemon juice
2 cups water
1 cup sugar (taste)
3 medium ripe bananas, sliced

#2 can pineapple chunks with juice
small bottle maraschino cherries chopped with juice

Mix all ingredients together. Pour into biscuit pan or pyrex pan. Freeze, stirring occasionally to prevent icing.

Mrs. H. Levy (Elsie)

WHIPPED JELLO DESSERT

2 small cans fruit cocktail
1 package cherry-flavored gelatin

½ pint whipping cream
chopped nuts

Drain fruit cocktail, save juice and use in place of water when making jello.

Make jello, place in refrigerator until soft but not firmly set.

Whip ½ pint whipping cream, fold in jello, then fruit cocktail, then nuts.

Return to refrigerator either in large bowl or individual dishes.

Serves 6 to 8.   *Mrs. Gene Burke (Jean)*

CAKES
and
COOKIES

B. Sartorius

APPLE COFFEE CAKE

½ cup nuts
2 teaspoons cinnamon
½ cup granulated sugar
½ cup butter or margarine
1 cup sugar
2 eggs

2 cups sifted flour
1 teaspoon baking powder
½ teaspoon salt
1 teaspoon baking soda
1 cup sour cream
1 medium apple, sliced

Mix nuts, cinnamon, and ½ cup sugar. Grease angel food pan and heat oven to 375°.

Cream butter and 1 cup sugar. Add eggs one at a time. Sift flour with salt, soda, and baking powder and add alternately with sour cream. Pour ½ batter into pan; top with sliced apples; pour in other half and top with nut mixture. Bake 40 minutes.

Serves 6 - 8.   *Mrs. Milton Schwartz (Betty Claire)*

APPLE PIE CAKE

½ cup shortening
2 cups sugar
2 eggs
2 teaspoons vanilla
2 cups flour
2 teaspoons baking soda
2 teaspoons nutmeg

2 teaspoons cinnamon
1 teaspoon salt
4 tablespoons hot water
5 cups diced apples (peeled &
  cored)
1 cup chopped nuts

Cream shortening and sugar together. Stir in eggs and vanilla. Sift together flour, baking soda, nutmeg, cinnamon and salt. Stir half of flour mixture into shortening. Beat in two tablespoons hot water and stir in remaining flour mixture; then remaining water, beating well after each addition. Stir in diced apples and nuts. Spread in 13" x 9" x 2" cake pan. Bake at 350° 45-50 minutes or until sides pull away from pan. Slice when cool.

Serves 24.   *Mrs. Edward J. Levy (Edna)*

APPLE SAUCE CAKE

1 cup apple sauce
½ cup peach jam
2 cups sugar
1 cup butter
2 eggs
3 cups sifted flour
2 teaspoons soda
2 teaspoons cinnamon

1 teaspoon ground cloves
1 teaspoon nutmeg
½ teaspoon salt
1 teaspoon vanilla
½ pound chopped dates
¼ pound chopped cherries
1 cup nuts

Cream butter and sugar. Add the eggs, then add peach jam. Combine flour with the spices. Dissolve soda in apple sauce. Add apple sauce alternately with the flour to the butter mixture. Add vanilla. Then add the dates, cherries, and nuts. Bake in greased and floured loaf pan for one hour at 350°.

Mrs. William Stool
Del Rio, Texas

BANANA CAKE

¾ cup butter
1½ cups sugar
2 whole eggs
1¼ cups riced or mashed
    bananas

¼ cup buttermilk
1 teaspoon vanilla
2½ cups cake flour
½ teaspoon baking powder
1 teaspoon soda

Sift dry ingredients together. Cream butter and sugar, add eggs one at a time, beating well until batter is light and fluffy. At a slow speed, alternate flour mixture with buttermilk to which have been added bananas and vanilla, beginning and ending with dry ingredients. Bake in 2 greased and floured cake pans at 375° about 35 minutes. A never fail cake, especially good with 7 minute icing.

Mrs. Si Sartorius (Bunny)

BLACK FOREST CAKE

10 egg whites
½ teaspoon salt
2½ cups sugar
3 cups whipping cream

2 cups toasted almonds (finely chopped)
5 - 1 ounce squares semi-sweet chocolate

Beat egg whites and salt until stiff. Gradually add 1½ cups of sugar. Beat until quite stiff. Make 3 - 9-inch circles on brown paper or wax paper. Divide mixture equally on three circles of paper. Bake in 250° oven for 2½ hours. Cool slightly and remove from paper. Melt 4 ounces of chocolate. Spread on cooled layers and allow to stand until chocolate is firm. Beat cream and add remaining sugar slowly. Gently fold in almonds. Frost layers with cream. Shave chocolate on top.

Given to *Mrs. Irvin D. Kaplan* (*Molly Ann*)
by *Mrs. Jerry Radoff*

BUTTERMILK CAKE

2 cups sugar
1 cup butter (2 sticks)
4 eggs
1 cup buttermilk

3 cups bread flour
1 teaspoon soda
1 tablespoon vanilla
1 tablespoon baking powder

Mix baking powder and soda with flour. Cream butter and sugar, add eggs one at a time and beat well. Add buttermilk alternating with dry ingredients which have been sifted together. Add vanilla. Pour in greased 8" x 12" x 2" pan. Bake at 350° about 45 minutes.

Syrup for top:
1½ cups orange juice

2 teaspoons grated orange rind
2 cups sugar

Mix ingredients, heat until sugar melts, and pour over hot cake. Leave cake in pan and cut in squares. Can be topped with whipped cream when served.

Mrs. Leon L. Block (*Era*)

BUTTERMILK POUNDCAKE

2 sticks butter or oleo
1 tablespoon shortening
2¾ cups sugar
5 eggs
1 cup buttermilk

3 cups sifted all purpose flour
pinch salt
⅓ teaspoon soda dissolved in 1
    tablespoon warm water

Let butter and shortening sit in mixing bowl at room temperature until soft; cream well with sugar; add eggs one at a time, and beat after each addition. Add salt to sifted flour and soda mixture to buttermilk. Starting with flour, add flour and buttermilk alternately, little at a time. Add vanilla and beat until batter is smooth. Bake in greased and floured tube pan at 325° for about 1½ hours.

Mrs. Leon Friedlander (Reba)

BUTTERMILK WHITE CAKE

3 cups cake flour
½ teaspoon baking powder
1 cup butter
2 cups sugar
2 eggs

½ teaspoon soda
1 cup buttermilk
1 teaspoon vanilla
1 teaspoon lemon extract
1 cup pecans, chopped

Sift and measure flour. Cream together baking powder and butter with flour. To this mixture add sugar, then eggs, one at a time, beating well after each. Dissolve soda in buttermilk and add vanilla and lemon extract. Mix in flour and milk alternately. Grease and flour a tube pan. Nuts may be placed on bottom of pan. Bake 1 hour at 325°.

Mrs. Rebecca Miller

THREE LAYER BUTTER CAKE

3 cups sifted cake flour
3 teaspoons baking powder
½ cup butter
1½ cups sugar

2 teaspoons vanilla
½ teaspoon lemon rind
3 eggs, separated

Sift flour 3 times. Sift together with baking powder. Cream 1 cup sugar and shortening together until fluffy. Add egg yolks one at a time beating after each. Then add vanilla and lemon rind. Add dry ingredients and milk alternately in small amounts mixing well after each addition, beginning and ending with flour. Beat egg whites until stiff but not dry. Add the remaining ½ cup sugar slowly to egg whites. Fold into batter. Pour into three 9" greased and floured pans and bake at 350° for 20 minutes. Spread orange filling between layers, cover top and sides of cake with chocolate fudge icing.

Orange filling:
½ cup sugar
3 tablespoons flour
4 teaspoons grated orange rind

1 cup orange juice
2 egg yolks
2 teaspoons lemon juice
pinch salt

Put sugar, flour and salt in top of double boiler and mix together thoroughly; add orange rind and juice, then butter and egg yolks and cook until smooth and thick. Remove from heat and add lemon juice. Allow to cool. Spread between layers of cake.

Mrs. I. S. Brochstein (Mildred)

CARROT CAKE I

5 eggs, separated
1 cup sugar
1 cup mashed cooked carrots

¾ cup blanched almonds, ground
grated rind and juice of 1 lemon

Beat egg yolks and sugar together until thick and lemon colored. Add almonds, carrots, lemon rind and juice, and blend thoroughly. Beat egg whites stiff, but not dry; fold into yolk mixture.

Pour into lightly greased 9 inch spring form pan. Bake at 350° for 40-50 minutes or until golden brown and set. Serve with whipped cream if desired.

Serves 8.   *Mrs. A. D. Schwarz (Lee)*

CARROT CAKE II

4 eggs, separated
2 cups sugar
3 cups flour
2 teaspoons soda in ⅓ cup
  buttermilk
½ cup salad oil
2 teaspoons cinnamon
1 teaspoon lemon extract
1 cup pecans
3 cups carrots, grated

Heat oven to 300°. Mix ingredients in order given. Fold in stiffly beaten egg whites. Bake for an hour or more in tube pan.

Topping:
½ cup orange juice
1 cup sugar
1 teaspoon grated orange rind

Mix well. Pour over cake as soon as it is taken from the oven. Let cool in pan.

Mrs. Leonard Gold (Selma)

CHEESE CAKE I

Crust:
¾ stick butter—3 ounces
1½ cups graham cracker
  crumbs

Melt butter in skillet; add crumbs until butter is absorbed. Line spring form pan with this mixture. Set aside.

Filling:
3 - 8-ounce packages cream
  cheese, softened
4 eggs
1 cup sugar
1 cup sour cream
pinch salt
1 teaspoon vanilla

Put all ingredients except eggs in mixer and blend well. Add eggs one at a time and mix well after each addition. Bake at 350° for 35 minutes. Cool; add glaze; refrigerate.

Glaze:
1 cup water
2 tablespoons cornstarch
½ to 1 cup sugar
red food coloring
fresh strawberries

Heat water, sugar and cornstarch until thick; stir frequently; add berries and coloring; cool. Pour on top of cake.

Mrs. Ronny Finger (Judy)
from *Mrs. R. R. Miller,* Phoenix, Arizona

CHEESE CAKE II

5 eggs, separated
1½ cups sugar
¼ cup flour
½ pint table cream

3 - 8-ounce packages cream
   cheese
juice of one lemon
1 tablespoon vanilla

Crust:
1 package zwieback (crushed
   not too fine)
4 tablespoons sugar

chopped nuts (optional)
2 sticks of butter or margarine,
   melted

Line spring form tube pan around bottom funnel and sides. Refrigerate.

Use electric mixer, keep running as you add all ingredients. Blend egg yolks with sugar and flour. Add table cream then crumble cream cheese into mixture. Add lemon juice when the mixture is smooth. Continue mixing. Add vanilla and remove from mixer. Fold in gently the stiffly beaten whites.

Pour mixture into crust and place in cold oven. Bake at 375° exactly 1 hour. Turn off heat, open door and let cake remain in oven another hour to cool.

Use imagination for toppings—sour cream, strawberries, a tart preserve, or I like lemon sauce with grated lemon rind in it. Even without topping, a delicious cake.

Serves 20-24.

Mrs. Glenn Epstein

CHERRY CAKE

2 slices candied pineapple
1 pound whole pecans
½ pound whole candied
   cherries
1 pound whole dates

1 cup sugar
1 cup flour
½ teaspoon salt
4 eggs, well beaten
1 teaspoon baking powder

Mix sugar, flour, salt, eggs and baking powder. Add fruit and nuts. *Do not mix fruit with flour.* Bake at 275° for 2 hours in ungreased angel food cake pan, which has been lined with wax paper.

Serves 8.

Mrs. Saul Friedman (Elaine)

COTTAGE CHEESE TART

Crust:
1 cup sugar
¼ pound butter, melted

cinnamon to taste
graham cracker or zwieback
  crumbs

Mix together and line spring form.

Filling:
3 cups cottage cheese, sieved
1 cup sugar
½ cup flour
4 eggs

1 - 6-ounce can evaporated milk
juice of ½ lemon
1 teaspoon vanilla
salt

Mix all ingredients in bowl. Pour into spring form and bake 1 hour at 325°. Do not open oven door until it is cool.

Mrs. M. M. May (Linda)

CREAM CHEESE TART

4 eggs, separated
1 cup sugar
10 packages (3 ounce size)
  cream cheese
1 cup milk

1 tablespoon melted butter
juice of lemons (takes at least 2)
2 tablespoons flour
pinch of salt
1 teaspoon vanilla

Cream egg yolks with sugar. Add cream cheese to egg mixture alternately with milk. Beat till smooth. Add butter, lemon juice, flour, salt, and vanilla. Beat egg whites stiff, and fold into cheese mixture.

Crust:
1 large box zwieback
melted butter

sugar
cinnamon

Crush zwieback into fine crumbs. Add butter, sugar, and cinnamon. Line a spring form with crust, and pour batter over crumbs. Preheat oven to 275°. Bake tart 1 hour, then turn off oven and leave tart in oven for 2 hours.

Topping:
1 large can unsweetened
  blueberries

1 cup sifted powdered sugar
1 tablespoon cornstarch
lemon juice

Drain juice into pan, and add sugar mixed with cornstarch, and lemon juice. Stir till thick, add berries. When cool spread over top of tart which has also been allowed to cool.

Serves 20.

Mrs. Sam A. Levy (Janis)

BURNT SUGAR CHIFFON CAKE

Burnt sugar syrup:
¾ cup sugar

1 cup boiling water

Melt sugar in heavy skillet over low heat until clear and medium brown. Remove from heat. Add boiling water. Stir over low heat until smooth.

2¼ cups cake flour
3 teaspoons baking powder
1 teaspoon salt (or less)
½ cup salad oil
5 unbeaten egg yolks
6 tablespoons water

1 teaspoon vanilla
6 tablespoons burnt sugar
  syrup
1 cup egg whites
¼ teaspoon cream of tartar

Sift dry ingredients together and make a well. Add remaining ingredients in center and beat until satin smooth. Add cream of tartar to egg whites and beat until very stiff. Fold batter into egg whites. Bake in unfloured 10 inch tube pan at 325° for 55 minutes, then 15 minutes at 350°. Invert pan one hour or until cool.

Mrs. Si Sartorius (Bunny)

CHERRY CHOCOLATE CAKE

½ cup butter
1 cup sugar
1 egg
2 one ounce squares unsweetened chocolate, melted
1½ cups sifted cake flour
1 teaspoon soda
¾ teaspoon salt
1 cup milk
¼ cup chopped maraschino cherries
2 tablespoons maraschino cherry juice
½ cup walnuts, chopped

Soften butter. Gradually add sugar, creaming until light and fluffy. Add egg and beat well; stir in chocolate. Sift together dry ingredients; add to the creamed mixture alternately with milk, a little at a time, beating smooth after each addition. Add cherries, syrup, and nuts. Grease bottom of 8x8x2 inch square pan; pour in batter.

Bake in moderate oven 350 degrees 40 minutes. Cool, frost with your favorite fudge frosting.

Serves 8. *Mrs. Jerry Rubenstein (Linda)*

CHOCOLATE CAKE

2 cups flour
2 cups sugar
1 stick oleo
½ cup shortening
4 tablespoons cocoa
1 cup water
½ cup buttermilk
2 eggs, beaten
1 teaspoon soda
1 teaspoon vanilla

Sift together flour and sugar. In saucepan melt oleo, shortening, cocoa and water. Bring this to a boil and pour over dry ingredients. Mix well. Add buttermilk, eggs, soda and vanilla. Bake in greased and floured 10″ x 15″ pan for 20 minutes at 400°.

Icing:
1 stick oleo or butter
4 tablespoons cocoa
7 tablespoons milk
1 box powdered sugar, sifted

Mix butter, cocoa and milk and bring to boil. Add the box of powdered sugar. Spread on cake.

Serves approximately 12. *Mrs. Alan Gold (Carol)*

CHOCOLATE CAKE — HEAVENLY HASH ICING

1¾ cups flour
½ teaspoon salt
1 teaspoon soda
1 cup milk
½ cup shortening

1¼ cups sugar
2 eggs
2 squares chocolate, melted
1 teaspoon vanilla

Cream shortening and sugar. Add eggs, one at a time. Add soda and salt to flour. Alternate milk and flour. Add vanilla and chocolate. Bake 20-30 minutes at 350 degrees in loaf pan 9" x 13."

Icing:
Melt 3 squares chocolate with 3
  tablespoons butter or oleo.
  Cool. Add 3 cups sifted

powdered sugar
⅛ teaspoon salt
7 tablespoons milk
1 teaspoon vanilla

Let stand until ready to spread. Spread sides. Then add 1 scant cup miniature marshmallows and 1 cup chopped pecans to icing in pan. Spread on top.

Mrs. M. M. Macow (Shirley)

NITA'S CHOCOLATE CAKE

1 stick butter
2 cups dark brown sugar
2 eggs
2 - 1 ounce squares bitter
  chocolate, melted

2 cups cake flour
1 teaspoon soda
1½ cups sweet milk
1 teaspoon vanilla

Cream butter and sugar, beat in eggs one at a time. Add sifted dry ingredients to creamed mixture alternately with milk. Add vanilla and chocolate. Beat on medium speed of mixer. Pour into greased oblong pan or two greased 9" pans. Bake at 350° for 25 minutes.

Serves 8-10.

Mrs. Sam Suravitz (Nita)

197

CLAIRE SCHRAM'S CHOCOLATE CAKE

1 stick butter
1 cup sugar
1¾ cups sifted cake flour
⅔ cup milk
1 cake German sweet chocolate

2 teaspoons water
1 teaspoon vanilla
2 heaping teaspoons tartrate
  baking powder
3 eggs, separated

Slice off just enough of the stick of butter to butter two small square cake pans. Cream remaining butter well with sugar. When lemon-colored add egg yolks one at a time. Then alternate flour with milk. Melt chocolate with water. Then add vanilla. Remove from mixer and add baking powder. Beat egg whites stiffly and fold in last. Bake at 350° for 25 minutes.

Icing:
5 cakes German sweet chocolate
2 squares bitter chocolate

¼ cup sugar
½ pint table cream

Place sweet and bitter chocolate in pot, add sugar and cream. When this melts it may appear to be curdled, but gradually adding more cream and beating by hand will make this the proper consistency for spreading between layers and on top and sides.

Mrs. DeWitt Grossman (Lois)

CHOCOLATE DATE CAKE

1 cup dates, chopped
1 cup hot water
1 cup shortening
1 cup sugar
2 eggs
1¾ cup sifted all purpose flour

1 teaspoon baking powder
1 teaspoon baking soda
2 tablespoons cocoa
1 cup semi-sweet chocolate bits
½ cup pecans, chopped

Mix dates and water and cool. Cream shortening and sugar. Add eggs and beat. Add all remaining ingredients except last two. Mix nuts and chocolate bits and sprinkle on top. Bake at 350° for 30 minutes.

Mrs. Melville May, Jr. (Linda)

CHOCOLATE FUDGE CAKE

1 stick of butter
1 cup sugar
4 eggs

1 - 8-ounce can chocolate syrup
1 cup flour
1 teaspoon baking powder

Cream butter and sugar. Add whole eggs, one at a time, beating well after each addition. Add syrup and fold in the flour sifted with the baking powder. Bake in greased 13" x 9" x 2" pan in a 350° oven for 28 to 30 minutes. This is a very moist cake. Do not over-bake.

Frosting:
½ stick butter
1 cup plus 2 tablespoons
   powdered sugar

1 egg
1 square bitter chocolate,
   melted

Cream butter, add sugar and egg and beat well. Add chocolate and mix. Spread on cake.

Mrs. Chester Brown (Rusty)

SABINA'S DEVIL'S FOOD CAKE

2 cups sifted cake flour
2 cups light brown sugar
2 eggs
3 squares bitter chocolate,
   melted

¼ pound butter
1½ cups milk
2 teaspoons vanilla
1 teaspoon soda

Pre-heat oven to 350°. Cream butter and sugar until fluffy. Add eggs one at a time beating after each. Add cooled chocolate and vanilla. Sift together flour and soda, add to batter mixture alternating with milk. The dry ingredients should be first and last. Grease and flour pans. For layer cake bake in two 9" pans for 20 minutes, or bake in loaf pan 9" x 13" for 45 minutes.

Ice with one minute chocolate fudge icing.

Sabina Weinstock

GERMAN CHOCOLATE POUNDCAKE

1 package (4 ounce) German
   sweet chocolate
2 cups sugar
1 cup butter
4 eggs

2 teaspoons vanilla
1 cup buttermilk
3 cups sifted all-purpose flour
½ teaspoon soda
1 teaspoon salt

Melt chocolate over hot water. Cool. Cream sugar and butter. Add eggs, flavoring and buttermilk. Sift together dry ingredients and add alternately with buttermilk until well mixed. Stir in chocolate until well blended. Pour batter into a greased and floured 9" tube pan. Bake at 300° about 1½ hours. Remove from pan. While still hot place under tightly fitted cover until thoroughly cool. Glaze is optional.

Glaze:
1 package (4 ounce) German
   sweet chocolate
1 tablespoon butter

¼ cup water
1 cup sifted confectioners' sugar
dash of salt
1 teaspoon vanilla

Melt chocolate and butter in water over heat. Combine sugar and salt in bowl. Gradually stir in chocolate mixture. Blend well. Add vanilla. Makes ¾ cup glaze.

Mrs. David Brand (Mollie)

COCONUT POUNDCAKE

1 cup shortening
2 cups sugar
6 eggs
2 cups flour

2 teaspoons baking powder
pinch of salt
2 tablespoons coconut flavoring
slivered blanched almonds

Cream shortening and sugar. Add eggs, beating after each. Sift and add flour, baking powder and salt. Add coconut flavoring and blanched almonds. Pour batter into well greased tube pan. Bake at 350° for 1 hour. Let stand 15 minutes to cool before removing from pan. Sprinkle top with powdered sugar.

Mrs. H. Levy (Elsie)

FUDGE CAKE (NEW ORLEANS)

1 stick butter
1½ squares bitter chocolate
1 cup sugar
½ cup cake flour

2 eggs
1 cup pecans, chopped
1 teaspoon vanilla

Sift flour and sugar together. Beat eggs. Add flour and sugar mixture, then pecans. Add previously melted chocolate and butter (over double boiler), and vanilla.

Spread in small square pan (8¼" x 8¼" x 2¼") lined with wax paper, not buttered. Cake should be very thick. Bake at 350° about 20 to 25 minutes. Should not be too well done.

Icing:
1 cup powdered sugar
4 tablespoons cocoa
¼ stick butter

1 teaspoon vanilla
enough milk or cream to
   moisten
chopped nuts

Melt butter; add cocoa, sugar and cream to make it thick enough to spread. Add vanilla. Ice heavily and top with chopped nuts. Not a brownie and not a slice of cake, but delicious.

Mrs. Simon M. Frank (Hank)

CHOCOLATE FROSTING

3 squares unsweetened
   chocolate
2 tablespoons butter
12 marshmallows
¼ cup water

dash of salt
2 cups sifted confectioners'
   sugar
1 teaspoon vanilla

Place chocolate, butter, marshmallows and salt in a saucepan. Heat over a low flame until melted and mixture is smooth. Remove from fire and beat in remaining ingredients.

Will frost layers, top and sides of a 9" cake.

Mrs. Richard Marks (Nonie)
Mrs. Etta Nathan

CHOCOLATE FUDGE ICING

| 2 cups sugar | ½ cup butter |
| ½ cup cocoa | ½ cup milk |

Cook all ingredients together in iron skillet until soft ball forms in cold water, or until it bubbles. Beat often while cooking. Remove from heat and beat until spreading consistency, about 5-10 minutes.

Mrs. Clara Loewenberg
Mrs. Gus Block (Gay)

HIGH AND HEAVENLY MARBLE CAKE

2 sticks margarine	2 cups cake flour
1½ cups sugar	2 teaspoons baking powder
4 eggs, separated	pinch salt
½ cup milk	½ cup chocolate syrup
1 teaspoon vanilla	

Cream margarine and sugar well. Add egg yolks and beat. Add dry ingredients alternately with milk and vanilla, beginning and ending with dry ingredients.

Fold in stiffly beaten egg whites. Pour into greased and floured tube pan, reserving approximately 3 cups batter. Mix chocolate syrup with reserved batter. Spoon chocolate mixture in four mounds on top of batter. Cut through mounds to make the marble, using a knife. Bake at 350° approximately 45 minutes.

Glaze:	2 tablespoons strong coffee
1 square bitter chocolate	1 cup powdered sugar
2 tablespoons margarine	½ teaspoon vanilla

Melt chocolate and margarine together. Remove from heat; add coffee, sugar and vanilla. Beat until consistency to pour over cake.

Mrs. I. B. Westheimer (Fannie)

COFFEE CAKE

2 cups flour
2 teaspoons baking powder
½ teaspoon salt
1½ cups sugar

½ cup butter
3 eggs
1 cup milk less 1 tablespoon
1 teaspoon vanilla

Sift flour, baking powder, salt and sugar. Cut in butter. Beat eggs and add milk, vanilla and beat into dry ingredients.

Streusel topping:
½ cup brown sugar
2 teaspoons cinnamon

2 tablespoons flour
½ cup chopped nuts
3 tablespoons butter, melted

Mix together until crumbly. Grease and flour pan; pour in batter and sprinkle with topping. Bake at 375° for 30 minutes.

Mrs. N. Levy (Tillie)

COFFEE CAKE

1 cup sifted sugar
1 stick butter
2 eggs
1 teaspoon vanilla

½ cup milk
1½ cups cake flour (sifted)
1 heaping teaspoon baking
  powder

Cream butter and sugar well. Add eggs one at a time. Then add vanilla, milk, flour, and baking powder. Put in greased pan and bake at 350° until done. (20 - 30 minutes)

Icing:
5 tablespoons butter
5 tablespoons light brown sugar

3 tablespoons cream
a few nuts

Cook sugar, butter, and cream together until melted. Add nuts and pour over cake while hot. Then place this under broiler until it bubbles.

Mrs. Sam Suravitz (Nita)

RAISIN-APPLE COFFEE CAKE

¾ cup sugar
¼ cup soft shortening
1 egg
½ cup milk
1½ cups sifted all-purpose flour
½ teaspoon salt

2 teaspoons double action
  baking powder
½ cup seedless raisins
apples, thinly sliced
1 teaspoon cinnamon
2 tablespoons sugar

Preheat oven to 375°. Mix together thoroughly ¾ cup sugar, shortening, and egg. Stir in milk. Sift together flour and baking powder and salt and add to batter. Stir in raisins. Spread batter in greased and floured 9" x 9" x 1¾" square pan.

Arrange thinly sliced apples attractively on top of batter, pressing them in slightly. Sprinkle top with cinnamon mixed with sugar. Bake 25 to 35 minutes at 375° until inserted toothpick in center of cake comes out clean. Serve warm.

Mrs. Charles Newman (Diane)

PARTY COFFEE CAKE

½ pound butter
1 cup sugar
3 eggs
1 cup sour cream
2½ cups flour, sifted
2 teaspoons baking powder
1 teaspoon baking soda

pinch salt
1 teaspoon vanilla
1 teaspoon lemon extract
Mixture:
1 cup nuts, chopped
½ cup sugar
1 teaspoon cinnamon

Cream sugar and butter; add eggs one at a time; add sour cream; mix in gradually flour to which soda and baking powder have been added; add flavoring. Then use half of batter in long narrow greased pan; sprinkle ½ of mixture and then top with rest of batter. Sprinkle balance of mixture on top and bake at 375° for 30 minutes or until done.

Mrs. Raymond Peltz (Lee)

MYSTERY MOCHA CAKE

¾ cup sugar
1 cup sifted flour
2 teaspoons baking powder
⅛ teaspoon salt
1 square unsweetened chocolate
2 tablespoons butter

½ cup milk
1 teaspoon vanilla
½ cup brown sugar
½ cup sugar
4 tablespoons cocoa
1 cup cold strong coffee

Mix and sift first four ingredients. Melt chocolate and butter together over hot water; add to first mixture; blend well. Combine milk and vanilla; add and blend well with other mixture. Pour into greased 8" x 8" x 2" pan. Combine brown sugar, cocoa, and sugar. Sprinkle over batter. Pour coffee over top. Bake in moderate oven 350° for 40 minutes. This is delicious served warm with ice cream on top.

Serves 6-8.

Mrs. Harold Gilbert (Jeanne)
and Mrs. A. D. Schwarz (Lee)

PASSOVER POTATO FLOUR CAKE

9 eggs, separated
1½ cups sugar
¾ cup potato flour

½ cup mixed orange and lemon juice
1 teaspoon orange rind

Line 8" x 10" pan with wax paper allowing paper to extend above pan about 1½ inches.

Beat egg yolks with sugar in large mixmaster bowl at medium speed about ten minutes. Continue beating and add potato flour and the fruit juice and rind. Beat five minutes longer. Lastly, fold in beaten egg whites. Bake in 300 degree oven about one hour and ten minutes. Turn out on flat surfaced tray or plate and remove wax paper.

Ice with boiled icing using orange for flavoring. Makes delicious strawberry shortcake.

Mrs. David Brand (Molly)

PASSOVER SPONGE CAKE

8 eggs, separated
¾ cup sugar
½ cup orange juice
½ cup Passover cake flour

½ cup potato starch
¾ cup sugar
pinch of salt

In mixer beat egg yolks until creamy, add ¾ cup sugar and orange juice. Sift flour and potato starch together twice and add to mixture. Beat egg whites and salt until stiff. Gradually add sugar. Fold into batter. Bake in tube pan 1 hour and 10 minutes at 325°.

Mrs. L. M. Landa, Jr. (Lois)
from Mrs. B. Sanford, Sioux City, Iowa

PESACH CAKE

1 cup pecans, chopped fine
5 eggs, separated
1 cup sugar

rind and juice of ½ lemon
½ cup sifted matzo cake meal

Beat yolks until light. Add sugar, then juice and rind of lemon. Add the cake meal, nuts, and fold in the stiffly beaten whites. Pour batter in 8″ square pan, wax paper lined. Bake in 350° oven about 30 minutes or until brown. May be served topped with strawberries and whipped cream or plain.

Mrs. Milton Gugenheim (Aileen)

JAM CAKE

1 cup butter
2 cups brown sugar
1½ cups strawberry jam
5 eggs, separated
3 cups flour
1 teaspoon soda

1 teaspoon each of cinnamon,
  cloves and allspice
1 cup buttermilk
1 square bitter chocolate,
  melted

Cream butter and sugar. Add egg yolks, jam and chocolate. Add cinnamon, cloves and allspice to flour. Dissolve soda in buttermilk and add alternately with flour to butter mixture. Beat egg whites and fold into batter. Bake in three layers in 350° oven until top springs back when touched. Ice with Seven Minute Icing.

Icing:
1½ cups sugar
2 teaspoons white corn syrup
⅓ cup water

2 egg whites
pinch of salt
1 teaspoon vanilla

Put ingredients in double boiler with water slightly boiling and beat with rotary beater for 7 minutes. May have to increase recipe to cover completely 3 layers and sides.

Mrs. H. Levy (Elsie)

FRUIT CAKE

1 pound shelled pecans
1 pound seedless raisins
1 pound pitted dates
1 pound crystallized pineapple
½ pound crystallized cherries
1 - 8-ounce bottle maraschino
    cherries and juice
½ pound English walnuts,
    shelled

½ pound Brazil nuts, shelled
1 pound flour (2 cups)
1 pound sugar
½ pound butter
6 eggs
2 teaspoons baking powder
1 teaspoon nutmeg
1 - 8-ounce glass bourbon
    whiskey

Chop nuts and fruits coarsely. Mix with a little flour, enough to keep mixture from sticking together. Have ready in separate bowl.

Cream butter and sugar; add whole eggs, one at a time. Add whiskey and flour alternately. Then add fruit and nut mixture. Mix well with a spoon.

Place in well greased and floured loaf pans ¾ full. Bake at 325° for 1 hour or longer until mixture leaves sides of pan.

Makes four two pound cakes.

Mrs. A. S. Baer (Doris)

TOASTED BUTTER PECAN CAKE

2 cups chopped pecans
1¼ cups butter
3 cups flour, sifted
2 teaspoons baking powder
½ teaspoon salt

2 cups sugar
4 unbeaten eggs
1 cup milk
2 teaspoons vanilla

Toast pecans in ¼ cup butter in slow oven. Stir frequently. Sift flour with baking powder and salt.

Cream remaining butter; gradually add sugar. Blend in eggs; beat well after each. Add dry ingredients alternately with milk, beginning and ending with dry ingredients. Stir in vanilla and 1⅓ cups pecans. Turn into three greased and floured 8″ or 9″ round layer pans. Bake at 350° for 25 to 30 minutes. Cool; spread frosting between layers and on top.

Butter pecan frosting:
¼ cup butter
1 pound powdered sugar

1 teaspoon vanilla
4-6 tablespoons evaporated
  milk or cream

Cream butter. Add powdered sugar, vanilla and evaporated milk or cream until of spreading consistency. Stir in remaining pecans.

Mrs. Stanley Kottwitz (Ginger)

SPONGE CAKE

7 eggs, separated
¾ cup cold water
1½ cups sugar
1½ teaspoons vanilla

1½ cups flour
½ teaspoon baking powder
¾ teaspoon cream of tartar
¼ teaspoon salt

Beat egg yolks 10 minutes, pour in water and continue to beat. Add sugar and vanilla. Gradually blend dry ingredients sifted together (flour, baking powder and salt). Beat egg whites with cream of tartar until stiff, and fold into above mixture. Bake at 350° in ungreased tube pan. Invert until cold.

Mrs. Leo Rose (Chickie)

PINEAPPLE-PECAN UPSIDE-DOWN CAKE

¼ cup butter
¾ cup brown sugar (packed
   tight)
2 to 2½ cups pineapple cubes
1¼ cups sifted cake flour
1 teaspoon baking powder
½ teaspoon salt

3 eggs
1 cup granulated sugar
1 tablespoon lemon juice
⅓ cup pineapple syrup
pecans
maraschino cherries

Melt butter in 9" skillet or upside-down cake pan. Add brown sugar, stir until just melted. Arrange pineapple, pecans and maraschino cherries in pan. Sift flour, baking powder, and salt together 3 times. Beat eggs until light and fluffy; add sugar gradually. Fold in lemon juice, syrup and dry ingredients alternately. Mix only enough to blend. Pour batter over fruit. Bake at 350° for 50 to 60 minutes. Cool slightly. Invert on serving plate. Serve with whipped cream.

Makes 8-9 servings.   *Mrs. Simon M. Frank (Hank)*

THREE LAYER SPICE CAKE

1½ cups sugar
2 cups flour
1 teaspoon soda
½ teaspoon each cloves, allspice, cinnamon

¾ cup shortening or butter
1 cup buttermilk
½ cup raisins
½ cup pecans, cut fine
3 whole eggs

Cream sugar and shortening. Add eggs and beat well. Sift all dry ingredients together three times. Add to mixture alternately with buttermilk. Bake in three layers at 350°.

Icing:
1½ cups sugar
¾ cup butter or oleo, melted

½ cup evaporated milk
1 teaspoon vanilla

Cook 10 minutes, stir. Take off heat and beat until proper consistency to spread on cake.

                    Mrs. H. Paul Levy (Norma)

MAMA'S OLD FASHIONED POUNDCAKE

1 pound butter
1 pound sifted cake flour
  (2 cups)

10 eggs, separated
2 cups sugar
1 teaspoon vanilla

Cream butter; work in flour until mixture is mealy; beat egg yolks, sugar and vanilla until fluffy; add butter and flour mixture gradually. Fold in stiffly beaten egg whites. Bake in two 4" x 8" loaf pans for 1¼ hours at 325°.

Mrs. Robert Rappold (Elizabeth)

VANILLA WAFER CAKE

2 cups sugar
6 eggs
2 small cans coconut
2 sticks margarine or butter

½ cup sweet milk
1 - 12-ounce box vanilla wafers
1 teaspoon vanilla
1 cup pecans, chopped

Crush vanilla wafers until fine. Cream butter and sugar and add eggs one at a time, beating after each; then milk, vanilla wafer crumbs, coconut, pecans, and vanilla. Bake in angel food cake pan 1 hour at 350°. Test with broom straw.

Mrs. Milton Robinowitz (June)

APRICOT BALLS

1½ cups dried apricots, ground
2 cups coconut flakes
⅔ cup sweetened condensed
  milk

1 tablespoon orange juice
1 teaspoon orange rind
powdered sugar

Mix ingredients well. Roll into balls and then roll in powdered sugar.

Makes 32.

Mrs. Manuel Bloom (Mitzi)

APRICOT BARS

1½ cups flour

1 teaspoon baking powder

1 cup brown sugar

1½ cups quick cooking oats

¾ cup butter

1 cup apricot jam

Mix flour, baking powder, brown sugar and oats. Cut in butter until crumbly. Pat ⅔ of mixture into a 13 x 9½ x 2 inch pan. Spread with jam. Cover with remaining crumb mixture. Bake in 350° oven about 35 minutes. Cool and cut in squares or bars.

Mrs. Joel Levy (Tudy)

APRICOT BROWNIES

⅔ cup dried apricots

½ cup butter

1 cup flour

¼ cup sugar

½ cup chopped nuts

⅓ cup flour

¼ teaspoon salt

½ teaspoon baking powder

2 eggs, well beaten

1 cup brown sugar

1 teaspoon vanilla

Rinse apricots, cover with water and boil 10 minutes. Drain, cool, and chop. Heat oven to 350 degrees. Grease square pan. Mix butter and granulated sugar and 1 cup flour until crumbly. Pack mixture into pan and bake 25 minutes or until light brown. While baking, sift together: ⅓ cup flour, baking powder, and salt. Gradually beat brown sugar into eggs, add flour mixture and mix well. Stir in vanilla, nuts and apricots. Spread over baked layer and bake 30 minutes. Cool, cut in squares and roll in powdered sugar.

Mrs. Glenn Epstein

BROWNIES

4 eggs
2 cups sugar
1 cup butter
1 cup flour

2 cups chopped pecans
4 squares unsweetened
chocolate
2 teaspoons vanilla

Cream butter and sugar. Add beaten eggs, flour and vanilla, melted chocolate and pecans. Bake at 325° in a biscuit pan. Frost with fudge icing.

Fudge Icing:
1 box powdered sugar
½ to ¾ stick butter

3 squares chocolate
dash salt
vanilla

Mix sugar with melted butter and chocolate. Add enough milk or cream to spreading consistency. Add vanilla and salt. Beat until creamy and frost brownies before cutting.

Mrs. Daniel Leibowitz (Joan)

BROWN SUGAR BROWNIES

¼ cup butter
1 cup brown sugar
1 egg
1 teaspoon vanilla
½ cup all-purpose flour (sift,

then measure)
1 teaspoon baking powder
½ teaspoon salt
½ cup nuts, chopped

Melt butter and brown sugar. Stir until dissolved. Cool slightly. Beat in the egg and vanilla. Sift the flour and then resift with baking powder and salt. Stir together and add chopped nuts. Pour into greased 8″ x 8″ pan lined with foil. Bake at 350° for about 30 minutes.

Mrs. Emile Zax (Bayla)

BUTTER ICEBOX COOKIES

½ cup butter
1 cup sugar
1 egg
1 teaspoon baking powder

1 teaspoon vanilla extract
2 cups (heaping) all-purpose
  flour

Mix all ingredients together. Roll dough in a ball and refrigerate either in freezer or icebox to chill. Roll dough on a floured board. Cut into different shapes. Place on a greased cookie sheet and put sugar and cinnamon on each cookie. Bake in 350° oven about 12 minutes until brown. Remove immediately to cake cooler.

Mrs. Leon Friedlander (*Reba*)

CHOCOLATE DROPS

1 egg
1 cup brown sugar
¼ cup butter and ¼ cup
  shortening
1½ cups of all-purpose flour
  (sift before measuring)

1 teaspoon vanilla
3 tablespoons cocoa
½ cup milk
1 cup nuts, chopped
1 teaspoon baking powder

(*Tip*: *Grease but do not flour pan.*)

Cream sugar and butter, then add egg. Add cocoa, milk, flour and baking powder (sifted together). Add nuts and vanilla. Drop by teaspoon and bake in 350° oven for 10-15 minutes. Ice with your favorite chocolate icing.

Mrs. William Stern (*Lucille*)

CHOCOLATE COOKIES

2 cups sugar
4 eggs
2 teaspoons vanilla
½ cup shortening, melted
4 squares chocolate, melted

2 cups flour
2 teaspoons baking powder
1 teaspoon salt
½ cup nuts, optional
powdered sugar

Beat eggs, sugar and vanilla. Blend chocolate and shortening; add flour. Chill overnight and then shape into balls and roll in powdered sugar. Bake in 325° oven for 10 to 12 minutes. Take out of oven sooner if a chewy cookie is desired.

Mrs. Raymond Brochstein (*Susan*)

COCONUT BARS

½ cup brown sugar
½ cup butter, melted

1 cup flour

Mix and spread on tins as you would pie crust. Bake until brown and cover with:

2 eggs
1½ cups brown sugar
1 cup nuts
½ cup coconut

1 teaspoon vanilla
2 tablespoons flour
½ teaspoon salt
¼ teaspoon baking powder

Bake again to golden brown. Cut in strips and roll in powdered sugar.

Mrs. Isadore Peal (*Carrie*)

CRYSTAL BARS

3 eggs, separated
1 cup sugar
¾ cup flour

1 teaspoon baking powder
1 cup chopped nuts
1 cup chopped dates

Beat eggs separately, add sugar to beaten yolks, add beaten whites, lastly fold in flour and fruit. (Do not over beat.) Bake in a 400° oven for about 12 minutes until lightly browned. Use large pan lined with wax paper. Cut into squares and roll in powdered sugar. Store in airtight can.

Mrs. Milton Gugenheim (Aileen)

DANISH COOKIES

1 pound butter	4½ cups flour—measured
9 tablespoons granulated sugar	after sifting
2 cups ground pecans	jelly

Mix all ingredients together, roll small quantity in balls the size of marbles. Make a depression in each and fill with jelly. Bake in a 350° oven until lightly browned. Put on waxed paper that has been sprinkled with powdered sugar, and when cool sprinkle tops with powdered sugar.

Makes 150.   *Mrs. Julie Dreyfus*

DATE-NUT BAR

1 cup pecans, cut fine	1 cup powdered sugar
1 cup dates, cut fine	1 teaspoon cinnamon
4 tablespoons flour—put over	½ teaspoon salt
dates and nuts	½ teaspoon nutmeg
2 eggs	4 tablespoons butter, melted

Beat eggs until lemon colored, add powdered sugar a little at a time, add cinnamon, salt and nutmeg.

In a small pan, 8 x 8 x 2, add four tablespoons of melted butter. Into the egg and sugar mixture add the flour, dates and nuts. Put into greased pan. Bake in a 325° oven for 20 minutes.

Yields 24 pieces.   *Mrs. Harold Gilbert (Jeanne)*

FRUIT CAKE BITES

1 cup brown sugar (packed)
¼ cup butter
2 large eggs
⅓ cup bourbon
1½ teaspoons soda dissolved in
    1½ teaspoons sweet milk
1½ cups flour, sifted
½ teaspoon nutmeg

½ teaspoon cinnamon
¼ teaspoon cloves, ground
1 pound dates, cut up
½ pound candied cherries, cut
    in halves
½ pound candied pineapple,
    chopped
1 pound pecans

Cream butter and sugar, add eggs and bourbon. Add soda and milk, alternately with dry ingredients. Add nuts and fruits. Mix *thoroughly*. Drop 1 teaspoon of mixture into paper candy cups. Decorate with candied fruit or nuts. Bake at 325° for 20 minutes.

Mrs. Ross Seline (Dee)

LIZZIE'S MINIATURE FRUIT CAKES

½ cup butter
1 cup brown sugar
4 eggs
6 ounces bourbon
3 tablespoons sweet milk
3 scant teaspoons soda

3 cups flour
1 teaspoon cloves
1 teaspoon nutmeg
1 teaspoon cinnamon
1½ to 2 pounds whole pecans
2 pounds mixed candied fruits

Dust ¼ of the flour over pecans and fruit to coat. Let stand. Cream butter, sugar, and eggs. Combine with bourbon. Add the milk and soda. Mix the rest of the dry ingredients together and add them to the mixture. Add rest of flour, nuts, and fruit. Drop by tablespoonfuls onto greased cookie sheet. Bake at 325 degrees for 30-45 minutes, until brown.

Makes 100-125.

Mrs. Jake B. Sampson (Pauline)

GUMDROP-COCONUT COOKIES

1 cup butter or shortening
1 cup brown sugar
1 cup white sugar
2 eggs, beaten
2 cups flour
¼ teaspoon salt
1 teaspoon soda
1 teaspoon baking powder

1 cup coconut, finely flaked
2 cups oatmeal
1 teaspoon vanilla
1 cup finely cut gumdrops
  (candied cherries or dates
  may be substituted)
½ cup nuts, chopped

Cream the butter, brown sugar and white sugar. Add the beaten eggs to the creamed mixture and blend well. Sift together the flour, salt, soda, and baking powder and stir into creamed mixture. Add coconut, oatmeal, vanilla, gumdrops and nuts. Drop from teaspoon onto greased cookie sheet, flatten with fork dipped in milk. Bake about 10 minutes in hot oven at 400°.

Mrs. Sam Robinson (Ruth)

HERMITS

¾ cup butter or oleo
1½ cups light brown sugar
½ cup molasses
3 eggs
4 cups cake flour, sifted
1 teaspoon salt
1 teaspoon cinnamon
1 teaspoon nutmeg

½ teaspoon cloves
½ teaspoon allspice
½ teaspoon mace
¼ cup strong coffee
1 cup nuts, chopped
1 cup each raisins and currants
powdered sugar, sifted

Cream butter and sugar until light. Beat in molasses. Add eggs, one at a time, beating thoroughly after each. Sift flour, salt, and spices; add to first mixture alternately with coffee, beating until smooth. Fold in nuts and fruit. Pour into 15" x 10" x 1" pan lined with waxed paper. Bake in moderate oven 350° about 20 minutes. Turn out on rack and peel off paper. Slip onto cutting board and cut. Sprinkle with powdered sugar.

Yields 35 bars.

Mrs. Robert E. Caine (Sunny L.)

GRAHAM CRACKER CRUMB COOKIES

2 cups graham cracker crumbs
1 - 10-ounce can condensed
 milk
1 small package semi-sweet

chocolate bits
1 cup pecans, chopped
1 teaspoon vanilla

Combine all ingredients except the nuts. Spread into a square 8 x 8 buttered pan. Top with nuts and bake in a 350° oven about 20 minutes. Let cool and cut in squares.

Makes 16 cookies.

Mrs. Sam Suravitz (*Nita*)

KICHEL

(The following recipe is called a "Kichel" by my husband's family. It could be of German origin. His mother made it for the family and since it was my husband's favorite, she taught me how to make it. It reads easy but takes practice in knowing when to "roll out" and when it is ready to remove from oven. We always serve it with tea, coffee or after the Sabbath dinner — like a dessert. Each person breaks off a piece as we pass it around the table.)

1 egg
¾ cup flour
½ cup salad oil

2 tablespoons sugar
dash of salt

Beat egg lightly with a fork. Add salt and then add sifted flour slowly until ready to roll out. Roll out dough to about ¼ inch thickness as you would for a pie crust. Cover a 9 inch pie plate with salad oil. Place dough into plate. Add more oil over the top of shell, sprinkle with sugar. Place on top rack of preheated 500° oven for 8-11 minutes. Remove when golden brown. Place at once on platter, pouring the oil off as you do so and sprinkle top again with sugar. Ready to eat when cool.

Mrs. Hyman Schachtel (*Barbara*)

LEMON SQUARES

1 cup flour
½ cup shortening
¼ cup powdered sugar
2 beaten eggs
2 tablespoons lemon juice

lemon rind
½ teaspoon baking powder
1 cup sugar
2 tablespoons flour

Mix together well—flour, shortening and powdered sugar. Put into 8 inch square pan and bake at 350° for 20 minutes.

Mix the eggs, lemon juice, rind of lemon, 1 cup sugar, 2 tablespoons flour, and baking powder. Pour this into baked crust. Bake at 350° for 30 minutes. Slice and cut into squares.

Mrs. Edward Levy (Edna)

LEBKUCHEN

4 eggs
2 cups dark brown sugar
½ teaspoon cloves
1 teaspoon cinnamon
½ teaspoon allspice

3 heaping tablespoons orange
   marmalade
4 tablespoons cocoa
1½ cups flour, sifted

Beat eggs with sugar, add remaining ingredients. Spread in a greased 13" x 9" pan. Bake in 325° oven for 30-40 minutes. Sprinkle pecans on top before baking.

Icing:
1 cup sugar   ½ cup cold water

Boil until icing spins a thread. Spread on top of cooled cakes.

Makes 75.   *Mrs. Morton Seline (Anita)*

OATMEAL COOKIES

1 cup sugar
1 cup butter
2 eggs
2 cups sifted flour
1 teaspoon soda

1 teaspoon each — cloves, nutmeg, cinnamon and allspice
1 teaspoon vanilla
1 cup oatmeal
1 package raisins

Cream sugar and butter. Add eggs and blend well. Add flour, soda, nutmeg, cinnamon, cloves, and allspice (sifted together). Blend. Add vanilla, oatmeal, and raisins. Blend. Drop by teaspoons on greased cookie sheet. Bake in 350° oven until done. Time: 10-15 minutes.

Makes 5 dozen.   *Mrs. Jerry Rubenstein (Linda)*

PASSOVER CREAM PUFFS

1 cup water
⅓ cup fat
1 cup matzo meal

½ teaspoon salt
4 eggs

Boil water and fat in saucepan. While boiling pour in salt and matzo meal. Continue cooking until it no longer sticks to sides of pan. Add unbeaten eggs, one at a time. Drop by spoonfuls onto cookie sheet. Bake 25 minutes at 450°. Reduce heat to 325° and bake 45 minutes.

Custard Filling:
2 eggs
¾ cup sugar
1 tablespoon potato flour

1 teaspoon butter
1 lemon
1 cup water

Beat eggs well, add sugar and flour, beating slowly. Add juice of lemon, butter and water slowly. Cook on top of double boiler until thick, stirring constantly. Use as filling for cream puffs.

Mrs. Simon Frank (Hank)

MATZO MEAL PECAN MACAROONS

2 egg whites, beaten stiff
1 cup sugar, added gradually
1 cup ground pecans

⅓ cup matzo meal
1 teaspoon cinnamon
grated lemon rind

Mix together, put in refrigerator for several hours. Roll into balls. Place on greased pan and bake 15 minutes in 375° oven.

Mrs. Albert Meyerson (Bertha)

PECAN CRESCENTS

½ pound butter
4 tablespoons powdered sugar
2 cups flour, sifted

1 teaspoon ice water
2 teaspoons vanilla
1 cup nuts, chopped

Mix well, roll into finger sticks or crescents. Bake in moderate oven 15-20 minutes.

Mrs. Albert Meyerson (Bertha)

PECAN STACKS

1 cup brown sugar
2 egg whites

2½ cups nuts, chopped
2 teaspoons vanilla

Add stiffly beaten egg whites to brown sugar. Then add chopped nuts and vanilla. Drop from a teaspoon onto a cookie sheet and bake slowly in a warm oven 325° to 350°. Time: 30-35 minutes.

Mrs. William Stern (Lucille)

PECAN SLICES

Sift before measuring: ½ cup butter
1 cup bread flour

Blend to smooth paste. Spread this mixture in 9" x 12" pan. Bake at 350° for 12 minutes.

Spread crust with following mixture:
2 eggs, beaten
1½ cups brown sugar
½ cup coconut

1 cup pecans, chopped
2 tablespoons flour
½ teaspoon baking powder
½ teaspoon salt
1 teaspoon vanilla

Bake at 350° for 25 minutes. When cool ice with 1½ cups powdered sugar thinned to spreading consistency with lemon juice. Cut into oblong pieces.

Mrs. Emile Zax (Bayla)

OLD FASHIONED TEA CAKES

½ cup shortening
½ cup sugar
1 egg
1 teaspoon vanilla

2 cups flour
2 teaspoons baking powder
2 tablespoons milk
cinnamon

Cream shortening and sugar. Add egg and vanilla. Sift flour with baking powder. Add to first mixture with enough milk so that you can roll dough on board. Cut with cookie cutter. Sprinkle a bit of cinnamon and sugar on top of cookie. Bake in greased pan in 350° oven until done. Roll dough rather thin.

A double recipe fills a gallon jar.

Mrs. Hermina Bettin

SAN FRANCISCO HOLIDAY CAKE

One of the following cakes:
Chiffon, sponge, or angel
food may be used

Crunch:
1½ cup sugar
¼ cup white corn syrup

¼ cup strong coffee
3 teaspoons baking soda (all
lumps removed)
1 cup almond halves
½ stick butter
salt

Stir all crunch ingredients except soda and bring to a boil. Cook to hard crack stage, 310° (or when a few drops break with a brittle snap in cold water). Remove from heat and add baking soda; stir vigorously until well mixed. Do not destroy foam by over-beating. Pour instantly into well-greased pan; *do not spread or stir.* Let stand until cool. Knock out of pan and crush between waxed paper into coarse crumbs. Brown almond halves in butter and salt lightly.

Filling:
1 quart heavy cream
2 tablespoons gelatin

8 teaspoons cold water
4 tablespoons sugar
2 teaspoons vanilla

Whip cream until slightly thick; add gelatin, which has been mixed with cold water and warmed over hot water until liquid; sugar, vanilla. Continue whipping until stiff.

Slice cake into four equal layers. Spread cream mixture between layers and on top and sides. Cover entire cake with crunch and browned almonds. Keep refrigerated until ready to serve.

Mrs. Frank Falkstein (Farnese)

SAND TARTS

½ cup powdered sugar, sifted
½ pound butter
2 cups cake flour, sifted

1 cup pecans, chopped
1 teaspoon vanilla

Mix all ingredients well. Shape into crescent shapes and place on ungreased cookie sheet. Bake at 350° for 20 minutes.

Mrs. Norman Schneidler (Barbara)

SHERRY BALLS

1 - 12-ounce box of vanilla
   wafers
1 cup pecans, chopped

1 cup powdered sugar, sifted
3 tablespoons light karo syrup
½ cup sherry wine

Roll wafers very fine. Add rest of ingredients. (This is very sticky.) Roll into very small balls. (They do not spread.) Place on wax paper on cookie sheets and refrigerate overnight.

Melt in a double boiler:
2 squares bitter chocolate

¾ large-size package Nestles
   dot chocolate

Melt these ingredients together and keep hot.

Take balls from icebox and cover with chocolate mixture —using toothpicks. Cover completely on all sides and put back in icebox.

Makes 100.

Mrs. Bernie Meyers (Arlene)
from Mrs. M. Berkovitz
Windsor, Canada

SPRITZ COOKIES

½ pound butter
1 cup sugar
1 egg

2½ cups flour, sifted
1 teaspoon vanilla

Cream butter and sugar. Beat in the egg, add vanilla, and then flour. Mix well. Put dough into cookie press and squeeze out on an ungreased cookie sheet. Bake in a 350° oven, until brown and crisp. Sprinkle with sugar and cinnamon or powdered sugar after they are baked and cooled.

Makes 100.

Mrs. Sam Suravitz (Nita)

STRUDEL

Dough:
¾ cup sugar
4 cups flour
4 teaspoons baking powder

1 teaspoon cinnamon
½ cup oil
¾ cup orange juice or milk
(approximately)

Sift dry ingredients into bowl and make a hole in center. Add oil and enough orange juice or milk to make a fairly moist pie dough. Divide into 4 equal sections. Roll out for thin pie dough, in long, narrow strips.

Filling:
½ package coconut
(about ⅔ cup)
1 cup pecans, chopped
½ box white raisins

1 - 12-ounce jar orange marmalade
1 pound pear honey or substitute thick preserves, chopped

Mix ingredients together and divide into 4 equal sections and spread on thin dough. Roll and bake at 325° for 45 minutes.

Mrs. Sol Roosth
Tyler, Texas

APRICOT CREAM CHEESE STRUDEL

1 - 8-ounce pkg. cream cheese
2 sticks butter or margarine
2 cups bread flour
apricot preserves

cinnamon
sugar
pecans
coconut, shredded

Blend well soft cream cheese and butter. Add flour and knead with hands. Form into large ball and wrap in wax paper and refrigerate until thoroughly chilled. Divide into three equal parts. Roll each as thinly as possible on lightly floured board. Spread apricot preserves over each oval sheet. Then sprinkle lightly with cinnamon and sugar, then pecans and lastly shredded coconut. Roll each as a log, making certain to fold the edges securely by pinching them tightly. Bake on ungreased cookie sheet for one hour at 350°. Cut while warm into ½ to ¼ inch slices. Sprinkle with powdered sugar. Store in covered container.

Mrs. Robert Reader (Gloria)

TAGELACH

4 eggs
1 tablespoon salad oil
½ cup orange juice
3 cups flour, sifted
1 teaspoon baking powder

pinch of salt
cinnamon
sugar
nuts

Beat eggs well for 10 minutes. Add oil and beat. Add orange juice and beat, add flour, baking powder, salt, mix lightly (do not over-handle dough). Cut in three parts. Sprinkle with cinnamon, sugar, and nuts. Roll. Twist and cut about 1 inch. Drop one by one in honey mix. Place in 375° oven—bake until brown.

Honey mix: Boil rapidly 2 cups of honey, 1 cup sugar, and ½ cup water. Boil for 15 minutes, covered, 10 minutes uncovered. Five minutes before through, add 1 tablespoon of ginger. Remove from fire. Add ½ cup boiling water to prevent sticking.

Mrs. L. A. Lewis (Esther)

TUTTI-FRUTTI COOKIES

(German-Yiddish Origin)

1 teaspoon baking powder
¼ teaspoon salt
1¾ cups flour
½ cup butter
½ cup brown sugar
2 eggs unbeaten
¾ cup pecans

¼ cup milk
3 cups cherries, crystallized
4 cups pineapple
2 tablespoons candied orange
  peel
2½ tablespoons orange extract

Sift dry ingredients three times. Cream butter, sugar and add eggs—then fruit and nuts, and flour and milk. Drop from a teaspoon onto a greased baking sheet. Bake 10 minutes at 400°.

Makes 5 dozen.   *Mrs. Robert Rappold (Elizabeth)*

MISCELLANY

ALMOND ROCA

1 pound sweet cream butter
12 ounces crushed pecans or
   almonds

2 cups granulated sugar
4 squares dark chocolate for
   candies

Melt butter till bubbly. Add two cups of sugar and almost all the pecans except a few to sprinkle over top of finished candy. Attach candy thermometer inside pan, turn burner to high, stir and cook till temperature reads 310°. Remove from heat and rapidly pour mixture into a one-half inch deep cookie sheet which is ungreased. Level off candy with a spatula. Melt the 4 squares of chocolate, spread over top of roca and sprinkle remaining pecans on top. Refrigerate. When cold, break candy into pieces.

Mrs. Jack Mott (Barbara)

DIVINITY SNO PEAKS

2 cups sugar
½ cup light corn syrup
½ cup hot water
¼ teaspoon salt

2 large egg whites, beaten stiff
1 teaspoon vanilla
candied cherries, quartered

Combine sugar, corn syrup, water, and salt in saucepan. Cook to hard-ball stage (248°). Slowly pour syrup in a thin stream over beaten egg whites, beating constantly. Beat till mixture holds shape. Stir in vanilla. Drop by heaping teaspoons onto wax paper, lifting and twirling spoon to form a peak. (I find a slightly buttered spoon helps.) If divinity becomes too stiff for twirling, add *a drop* or two of hot water to bring back to desired consistency. While peaks are still moist, decorate with candied cherries if desired. You may omit twirling process and add 1 cup coarsely chopped nuts and drop from spoon.

Mrs. Ross Seline (Dee)

KISSES

3 egg whites
1 cup sugar

2 cups pecans
1 teaspoon vanilla

Beat egg whites very stiff. Add sugar and vanilla, beat well and add pecans. Drop with teaspoon on a well greased pan. Bake in 300° oven for 45 minutes.

Makes 30.

Mrs. Abe Marks
by Mrs. Saul Friedman (Elaine)

DATE ROLL

2½ cups sugar
1 cup milk

½ pound dates
¾ cup chopped nutmeats

Cook sugar, milk and dates to soft ball stage (235° to 240° when using candy thermometer). Stir as needed to prevent burning. Remove from fire and cool to slightly more than lukewarm. Beat until it begins to harden. Add nuts and turn onto a damp cloth. Shape into a roll. Let stand until firm. Cut into slices as needed. This candy may be kept for some time if tightly covred.

Mrs. H. Paul Levy (Norma)

FUDGE

2½ cups sugar
2 tablespoons cocoa

1 cup light cream
2 tablespoons butter

Stir ingredients until well blended and continue until sugar is melted. Boil until it forms a soft ball in cold water or 228° on candy thermometer. Cool, then beat mixture until right consistency to spread. Nuts may be added when removed from fire.

Mrs. Simon Frank (Hank)

BUTTERMILK PRALINES

Combine in large pot:
2 cups white sugar
1 teaspoon soda
1 cup buttermilk

dash of salt
2 tablespoons butter
2 cups pecans

Boil until soft ball will form in cold water. Add 2 tablespoons butter and 2 cups pecans. Remove from heat and beat until creamy. Drop by tablespoon onto buttered tin pan.

Mrs. Philip Adelman
Sent by Mrs. Ralph Davidson (Mae)

CREAMY PRALINES

1 cup white sugar
2 cups brown sugar
¾ cup condensed milk
1 tablespoon white corn syrup

1 tablespoon butter
½ teaspoon vanilla
1 cup pecans

Combine first four ingredients in double boiler. Boil, stirring constantly, until a drop will form a soft ball when dropped in water. Remove from heat and add butter and vanilla, then pecans. Beat entire mixture until it begins to lose its gloss. Drop by teaspoon on wax paper.

Mrs. Arnold Miller
Waco, Texas
Sent by Mrs. John Landa (Nancy)

231

ROCKY ROADS CANDY

2 - 9¾-ounce (the large ones)
  plain Hershey bars
1 - 15-ounce can condensed
  milk

3 cups chopped nuts
1 large bag regular size marshmallows cut in half

Melt chocolate bars in double boiler. When melted, add milk and nuts. Line a 9″ x 13″ pan with wax paper. Pour half the chocolate mixture on bottom of pan, then add marshmallows and add chocolate mixture on top. Put in refrigerator overnight.

Turn upside down, peel off paper and cut into squares.

Mrs. Abner Burg (Bess)

ALMOND TOFFEE

1 cup chopped or slivered un-
  blanched almonds
1 cup butter (½ pound)
1 cup white sugar
⅓ cup brown sugar

10 almond Hershey bars
  (5 cent size)
2 tablespoons water
½ teaspoon soda
sprinkle of salt

Sprinkle half of almonds on buttered 9″ x 13″ pan. Melt butter in 2 quart heavy pot, add sugar and water, and mix well. Bring to boil, stirring constantly, and cook to hard crack stage, using a candy thermometer. Working fast, remove from heat and stir in soda. Pour carefully over almonds in pan. Spread Hershey bars over candy and put remaining almonds on top. Can turn over after being refrgierated and put chocolate mixture and nuts on both sides. Break in pieces with point of butcher knife.

Mrs. Max Wagner (Minna)

DILL PICKLES

22 cups water
1 cup vinegar
1 cup salt
cucumbers (very small)

garlic
red pepper or little hot peppers
dill
alum

Boil water, vinegar and salt. Pack jars with dill, cucumbers, garlic, dill, cucumbers garlic and ending with dill on top. Add a pinch of alum to each jar. Fill with hot solution and seal immediately. After sealing, turn upside down over night. Reverse, seal tighter, if possible.

Mrs. Walter Pye (Bessie)

MIXED PICKLES

2 quarts of vinegar
1 cup water
½ cup salt
¾ cup sugar
1 dozen small hot green peppers

1 teaspoon red pepper
1 head cauliflower
1 head cabbage
5 pounds pearl onions

Boil first 6 ingredients. Wash and break up cauliflower. Wash and cut up cabbage about 2 inches square. Peel and wash onions.

When solution boils, add vegetables and cover. Let stand over night and pack in jars and seal.

Mrs. Walter Pye (Bessie)

RAW CRANBERRY RELISH

1 quart cranberries
2 apples (core but do not peel)
2 oranges (peel and core)

2 cups sugar
½ orange, grated peel

Put all fruit through medium food chopper (not too fine). Add sugar and stir. Set in refrigerator for at least 12 hours. Will keep well for one or two weeks.

Mrs. H. Levy (Elsie)

FRESH GARDEN RELISH

2 large fresh peeled tomatoes,
   diced
1 peeled cucumber, diced
½ cup green pepper, diced
⅓ cup onion, finely chopped

2 tablespoons brown sugar
⅓ cup vinegar
1 teaspoon salt
½ teaspoon celery seed
½ teaspoon black pepper

Combine all ingredients and mix lightly. Chill several hours. Makes about 3 cups.

Mrs. Thomas Freundlich Jr. (*Cecile*)

PEPPER HASH RELISH

12 red sweet peppers
12 green sweet peppers
6 medium onions
1 tablespoon salt

2½ cups sugar
1 quart cider vinegar
2-3 tablespoons mustard seed

Grind peppers and onions together. Pour scalding water over them and let stand until lukewarm, then drain. Boil vinegar, sugar, salt, mustard seed, and ground peppers. Cook about 15 minutes. Put in jars and seal while hot. Makes about 6 pints.

Mrs. Charles Strauss (*Betty*)

SAUERKRAUT RELISH

1 quart can sauerkraut chopped
   fine
1½ cups sugar
1 cup vinegar

3 green peppers, chopped fine
3 onions, chopped fine
½ tablespoon celery seed

Drain kraut well. Mix all ingredients and let stand in covered container 2-4 hours. Keeps well.

Mrs. Thomas Freundlich, Jr. (*Cecile*)

PEAR (INDIA) RELISH

4 quarts hard pears, peeled
12 large red and green bell
   peppers

6 medium onions
6 long hot peppers

Grind and salt heavily. Let stand one hour or more. Rinse through
2 ice waters, squeeze well.

1 quart vinegar
4 cups sugar
1 tablespoon turmeric

2 tablespoons white mustard
   seed
2 tablespoons celery seed

Let all come to boil and boil two minutes. Bottle and seal immediately.

Mrs. G. Frank Lipper (*Nanette*)

WATERMELON RIND PRESERVES

Excellent with lamb and beef roasts.

1 melon rind
1 tablespoon lime
2 cups sugar

½ sliced lemon
2 sticks ginger

Pare green and pink from inch cubes of one melon rind. Soak overnight in one quart water and one tablespoon lime. Rinse well. Boil
in clear water 15 minutes. Drain. Boil one quart water, two cups
sugar, one-half sliced lemon and two sticks ginger for five minutes.
Add rind and cook till clear. Let stand overnight. Reheat and seal
in sterile jars.

Mrs. Robert Rappold (*Elizabeth*)

CRANBERRIES (Jellied)

1 box cranberries
sugar

juice of ½ lemon

Wash cranberries and put in large pot. Cover with water, not too much as cranberries float. Boil with cover until all berries have popped. Strain thru large strainer. Measure juice. Use ½ amount of sugar as juice. Add juice of ½ lemon. Bring to boil about 20 minutes or until syrup drops heavy from spoon. Rinse mold with cold water but do not wipe. Pour in cranberry jelly and when cold, place in refrigerator. You may make this as far as three days before. Keeps in refrigerator indefinitely. Serve with turkey.

Mrs. Abe Zuber (Stella)

———◆◆———

EGG NOG

12 eggs separated
1½ cups whiskey

1½ cups sugar
1 quart whipping cream

Beat egg yolks for 20 minutes. Slowly add whiskey to beaten yolks. Beat egg whites and slowly add sugar to beaten whites. Combine with yolks. Fold in whipped cream. Sprinkle with nutmeg.

Serves 15 to 20.

Mrs. Sam Levy
Sent by Mrs. Lionel Weil (Cecil)
Montgomery, Alabama

COFFEE PUNCH

1 gallon strong coffee
ice cream balls

1 quart syrup (1 cup of water to
1 cup of sugar)

Add syrup to coffee and chill thoroughly. When ready to use, pour over balls of ice cream (be generous). Pour into chilled punch bowl.

Mrs. B. G. Winner (Irene)

PARTY PUNCH

2 large cans frozen orange juice
2 large cans frozen lemonade
1 small can frozen lime juice

1 can water to each can frozen juice
1 - 48-ounce can pineapple juice

Mix each can juice and water in blender while still frozen. Add pineapple juice. Put in refrigerator in covered jars. May be made a day or two ahead. When ready to serve add:

¼ cup apricot cointreau or brandy
1 pint orange sherbet

2 large bottles orange soda water

TEA PUNCH (FOR LARGE GROUPS)

4 tablespoons tea
1 quart boiling water
4 cups sugar
3 cups water
1½ dozen lemons

1 dozen oranges
2 #2 cans crushed pineapple
1 quart maraschino cherries
2 quarts ginger ale

Put tea in quart boiling water and let stand 5 minutes. Strain. Boil sugar in 3 cups of water for 5 minutes. Add juice of lemons, oranges, crushed pineapple, and cherries. Just before serving, add ginger ale.

This is very inexpensive and good for young groups.

Mrs. Frank Falkstein (Farnese)

ICE RING

(To float in juices)

Put plain water (no coloring) in a 1 or 2 quart mold. Arrange red and green cherries, Mandarin oranges, etc. in mold. Freeze well. Put in punch bowl. Add sherbet to center of ring.

Chill punch bowl 3 or 4 hours ahead. Put ice cubes in plastic bag inside a pan and place in punch bowl. Cover top of bowl well with plastic wrap.

Serves 50-60.   *Mrs. Jake B. Sampson (Pauline)*

INDEX

STARCHES

VEGETABLES